Unblocking Organizational Communication

A companion volume to
50 Activities for
Unblocking Organizational Communication

Dave Francis

Gower

Published by
Gower Publishing Company Limited,
Gower House,
Croft Road,
Aldershot,
Hants GU11 3HR,
England

Reprinted 1989

British Library Cataloguing in Publication Data

Francis, Dave
   Unblocking organizational communication.
   1. Communications in management
   2. Communication in organizations
   I. Title
   658.4'5   HD30.3

   ISBN 0 566 02572 8

Printed and bound in Great Britain
by the Camelot Press Ltd, Southampton

Contents

Preface

Unblocking Organizational Communication is written for several audiences. First, those who occupy leadership roles; secondly, specialists in the growing field of planned organizational change; and lastly, I hope that those in the bowels of organizations may light upon this book and use it as a spur to encourage their seniors to reform.

The theory which underlies this book has been tested in several countries. Much of the original development work was completed in the USA and Canada, and I would like to thank Murray Dalziel of Boston, Roger Harrison of Berkeley, California, Henry Mintzberg of Toronto, and Ginny Goodfield of Marin County, California for their help and guidance.

No one could write a book in a field so well documented as this without drawing on the ideas of others. Where I am aware of the source of concepts and techniques I have given credit in the text. Some of the ideas in this book were developed with Don Young in Cyprus and I recall with great pleasure our long relaxed conversations which helped me develop my thinking. My writing style has been greatly influenced by my friend Mike Woodcock. My daughter, Samantha, made a major contribution with support, critique and secretarial help. My interest in organizational communication was first aroused by an action learning programme sponsored by Plessey Marine Ltd., which brought together Dave Downer, John Halstead, Chris Hennah, Geoff Main and Trevor Prince. I also thank Ezra

Kogan, Terry Hutton, Carol Bradshaw, Warner Burke, Meredith Belbin, Bob Tozer, Mark Walters, and Jane Cranwell-Ward for their counsel and support. These consultants and managers tackled the problems of business communications with vigour, tenacity and imagination. Without them this book would not have been written.

DF

Introduction

'Communications are terrible' – this is probably the most widespread complaint of those working in organizations.

There are many examples of failures in organizational communication. Senior managers burn the midnight oil to develop a new strategy for corporate survival, but are thwarted when the workforce react with cynical indifference. Departments that should co-operate are plagued by hostility that stubbornly persists year after year. Workers describe their company as practising 'mushroom management' – 'They keep us in the dark and periodically pour manure over us'. Many businesses have neglected to understand fully their competitors and customers, and have gone into bankruptcy as they serve yesterday's markets. Countless soldiers have died on the basis of misunderstandings. Such communication breakdowns are repeated thousands of times daily.

Almost everyone would proclaim that good communication is important. The topic is a regular feature of top management conferences and the subject of uplifting articles in corporate newspapers. But if we enquire, 'What exactly do you mean by good communication?' the reply is usually evasive and uncertain. Many managers lack a systematic framework to relate organizational performance to human communication.

This book is devoted to providing a systematic answer to the question: 'What exactly do you mean by good communication?' It will attempt to demystify a hazy and complex topic.

Introduction

The book has four objectives:

○ to provide a readable introduction to the field of organizational communication
○ to explore the concept of blockages to effective communication
○ to provide the theory which is one part of a planned programme for communication improvement
○ to inspire the reader to think about the potential of human communication in new ways.

The case for achieving excellent communications was put most persuasively by leading industrialist Michael Edwardes, who wrote:

> A key part of a successful manager's role is to communicate first and foremost to his workforce, to explain and to motivate, but he should also be prepared to take his arguments and judgements to a wide audience...Industry has to work very hard at improving the communication skills of its managers...Communications are becoming more complex and more efficient, for their technology is almost unlimited in scope. (*Back from the Brink*, Collins, London, 1983.)

This book argues that managers must change their thinking about organizational communication and stop perceiving it as a worthy but tedious duty. Rather, communication should be seen as the means by which managers:

1 Share the Compelling Vision (so that everyone knows what is important).
2 Integrate the Effort (so that human energy and resources all drive in the same direction).
3 Sustain a Healthy Community (so that people are working for the organization, not against it).
4 Make Intelligent Decisions (so that the organization reacts wisely to threats and opportunities).

These are the four purposes of organizational communication, which form the basis of the theory explored in this book. But the approach is neither conceptual nor impractical. A manager may say: 'Our business is hurting because we can't get communication right. It's not a matter of equipment but behaviour. I don't have three years to read all the research. I won't spend a fortune on fixing the problem, but I will devote reasonable effort. Tell me what I should do.' *Unblocking Organizational Communication* is an attempt to solve this real and important problem. This book translates these concepts into practical guidelines which provide the basis for a management-driven communication improvement programme.

The focus of this book is the organization, not the individual. It is useful to define terms briefly. An 'organization' is 'any identifiable group which has a largely autonomous management structure who produce defined goods or services'. Communication is defined as 'the medium through which managers lead, direct the activities of others, harness human creativity, co-ordinate specialists and control activities, and understand the needs and wants of those who work within the organization and those who use the organization's goods or services'.

In the book I interpret 'communication' widely. Spoken and written words are only one aspect of real communication. Perhaps most important are the actions or inactions of powerful people. An example illustrates the point. A new chief executive joined a large organization which was riddled with easy living and nepotism. She made two early decisions: to ban alcohol in the management dining room and to insist that all candidates for senior positions were psychologically tested. Both executive actions told people that things were changing; the organization began to 'shape up'. Few words were spoken, but communication had taken place. As the adage puts it, 'actions speak louder than words'.

The theory of purposeful communication described in this book is appropriate for single organizations like businesses, separate units, hospitals, large departments, factories, research facilities and so on. Large decentralized organizations should consider their individual enterprises separately. Many of the examples come from the business world, but the concepts apply to every kind of organization.

One note of caution: organizational communication patterns differ according to the size of the enterprise and the manufacturing technologies used. The approach described in this book has proved relevant in business, government, health care, service and military organizations. However, users should adapt the concepts to their own organization's culture and corporate style.

Many examples of organizations and individuals are given throughout the book. Where these are drawn from the personal experience of the author the names have been changed to maintain anonymity.

This book is based on the premise that organizations should be developed as a whole and it is important to introduce the concept of organizational development at this stage. Learning is not confined to individuals. Organizations can 'learn' to become better at communicating, therefore more focused, integrated, healthy and intelligent. Consider an example. The senior manager of a large telecommunications company told me: 'Eight years ago we had a captive market as almost everything we made went to the national telephone company. We were simply a manufacturing business. Now we have to compete world wide. We've looked very hard at what we do and what we weren't doing well enough. We had to learn to innovate and then market new products. It was a hard struggle to change, but it is a very different business today. Everybody's changed. There are new systems. We think differently.'

This manager wisely thought of his organization as a whole 'system' and, from his comments, we can deduce six key features which enabled organizational development to take place:

1   There was a real need for change.
2   People with power recognized that change was required.
3   A thorough diagnosis was carried out.
4   Difficult factors were dealt with.
5   There was a clear definition of aims.
6   Tenacity was shown (to keep working on the problems).

Each of these features is important and they are all interlinked. Communication improvement is an essential part of an organization development programme.

However, there is a note of caution. Despite their merits, the written prescriptions for organizational development are never sufficient. Organizations are living entities. It is impossible to study organizational communication with mechanical precision. If the writer presses the correct sequence of keys on a word processor then the text is moved in a predictable way. Organizations do not respond like machines; emotion, energy and willpower all play a vital part. Because of this, the reader is advised to use this book as a guide, not a gospel. The concepts and suggestions will help you to think systematically about organizational communication, but any improvement programme must be based on your interests, beliefs and commitments.

This book is based on the 'blockage' notion – a useful concept from 'Gestalt' psychology which suggests that an organization can be compared to a plumbing system with an interlinked pattern of pipes. Maximum effectiveness comes when the pipes are unblocked. Blockages affect the whole system and reduce overall effectiveness. How to improve the system? Simple: reduce or eliminate the blockages, which means:

○ blockages must be clearly identified
○ blockages must be explored, so try to understand them
○ the damage caused by blockages must be understood
○ a strategy of change should concentrate on unblocking – work intensively on clearing a few blockages, and don't spread your energy too thinly.

Effective communication is vital to those who have the privilege and the pain of holding leadership roles. Aims and objectives remain 'pie in the sky' unless they are persuasively communicated. Although senior executives may not have the time to implement personally a communication improvement programme, they can delegate this task to staff specialists or action teams. Three ingredients are necessary for a good chance of success. Firstly, senior management must give informed support. Secondly, a defined individual (or team) must be given a clear mandate and resources to complete essential diagnostic and planning work. Lastly, management must actually implement changes and persist despite difficulties.

This book does not delve into the technology of communication – digital codes, teleconferencing, international computer protocols and the like. There is already abundant attention on the vehicles and mechanics. We are concerned with purposeful communication – people working together to get things done.

Unblocking Organizational Communication is part of an integrated approach to improving organizational communication. Another book and a survey complete the 'package'. The companion volume, *50 Activities for Unblocking Organizational Communication*, provides practical tools for facilitating change. For those who wish to undertake a diagnostic survey, 'The Audit of Communication Effectiveness' is published separately. This is a validated instrument for evaluating blockages in organizational communication based on the conceptual model described in this book. Further details are available from Richmond Consultants Ltd, P.O. Box 67, Richmond, Surrey TW10 6PX, England, and Richmond Associates, 7 Schirmer Road, West Roxbury, MA 02132, USA. The two books and 'The Audit of Communication Effectiveness' enable a wide-ranging communication improvement programme to be undertaken.

What is communication?

The four purposes of communication

As part of the research for this book, I asked a group of experienced senior managers: 'Why is communication important?' These are some of their answers:

○ saves time
○ gets people pulling in the same direction
○ makes it easier to introduce changes
○ enables people to use their intelligence
○ gives people the information they need to do their jobs
○ helps me control what is going on
○ reduces the chance of enormous blunders
○ part of the responsibility to employees
○ shows people what they do is worthwhile.

The comments are interesting. They show that experienced managers perceive communication as a creative tool, not a mundane chore. They know from years of experience that qualitative factors like human communication are vital, although they are obstinately difficult to measure.

It is impossible to conceive of any organization operating without communication, just as we cannot imagine a human being living without a blood supply. We are right to assert that 'an organization is a collection of inert resources brought alive by communication'.

Some managers have regarded communication as a worthy but dull duty; part of the welfare requirement of running an organization. This attitude must be eradicated. It prevents managers from realizing that communication is the only way to channel human energy.

Communication is a key ingredient in high-performing organizations. This was shown vividly by the transformation in the performance of a British company, Jaguar cars. At the end of the 1970s, Jaguar's reputation was a disgrace. Dealers tried to complete sales on Friday to allow time for the trade-in car to be sold over the weekend before the disgruntled customer returned on Monday to call off the deal. Standards of workmanship of this allegedly luxury car often fell below mass-production vehicles. In 1980 leadership changes were made and the new chief executive, John Egan, led a remarkable programme of change. Four years later there was a long queue of customers, and quality problems were largely solved.

Each step in the recovery of Jaguar cars required excellent communication – rightly seen by management as a primary tool. John Egan talked persuasively and frequently to all employees. Simple but profound messages were echoed by managers. Mediocrity was not tolerated. A positive and outgoing, almost 'macho' leadership style was adopted. Up-to-date methods of communication drove the messages home. Every employee knew the unpleasant facts and what had to be done to survive. In 1980, Jaguar cars had almost gone over the brink and become a bankrupt company with an honourable history but no future. Exploiting the power of communication provided the means to bring about an almost unprecedented change of business fortunes.

The Jaguar case is important for another reason. It shows us that communication should be more than the occasional memorandum pinned to a grubby notice board. John Egan realized that an organization is a community of people which operates on an emotional level. He had to touch the hearts and minds of thousands of people. Jaguar, like all organizations, had evolved a distinct character (an organizational culture) which influenced the attitudes, thoughts and behaviour of all those who operated within it. Once established, an organizational culture becomes a strong informal code of conduct. Low standards had become accepted in Jaguar's culture.

John Egan understood that his communication strategy had to influence the corporate culture and ruthlessly destroy the self-destructive attitudes which were bankrupting the company. Communication which failed to influence underlying attitudes would not succeed. Invisible but powerful forces would neutralize his best efforts.

The Jaguar example shows us that organizational communication must be purposeful. It should enable managers to manage, leaders to lead and organizations to be integrated. Communication is not a substitute for management, leadership or organization, but the means by which these capabilities are exercised. We pay much attention to clever electronic gadgets which facilitate communication, but we often fail to exploit the potential benefits of this wizardry. We need to focus attention on communication for a purpose: the pursuit of organizational achievement.

Some organizations achieve more than others. Why? Performance is the result of the extent to which human energy is focused, specialists' efforts are integrated, a healthy community is sustained and intelligent decisions taken. These are the four purposes which are the basis for the theory of organizational communication developed in this book, as shown in the diagram.

The four purposes of communication

The remainder of this chapter describes these four purposes. Notice that there are three key words relevant to each category. These are the 'components' of organizational communication. More about this in the next chapter.

Communication for sharing the compelling vision

Communication is the medium through which managers give direction and sustain dynamism. Organizations, like people, have a personality or culture embedded in systems, attitudes, relationships, structures and policies. Organizational cultures tend to be passive. Something else is needed – a compelling vision – which is the corporate identity expressed in ways that excite people.

Clarity about a vision of the future can only come from the top. Without it organizations run down like Christmas toys with exhausted batteries. Consider how an original idea from an exceptional leader becomes an energizing focus which guides the growth of an organization. This is a compelling vision in action. When leaders lose their drive the organization is thrown into crisis.

It is communication that conveys the vision of the future to everyone within an organization. Communication brings vision, hope, direction, value, importance and meaning in a language that can be understood. It provides the emotional glue that binds people together, and touches something deep within each individual.

Sharing the compelling vision requires:

Alertness	everyone in the organization is sensitive to its external environment so that they can keep up to date, detect opportunities and foresee threats.
Focus	top management have a vision of the future which is so attractive that it compels people to want to help make it happen.
Attraction	managers persuade people throughout the organization to strive for corporate success.

Communication for integrating the effort

Much communication is concerned with integrating the efforts of different people to get complex things done. Imagine the co-ordination required to get an airliner from New York to London, maintain electronic surveillance of the USSR or launch a space station. Vast numbers of specialists must make their contributions at the right time. Suitable mechanisms must be created for co-ordination between individuals, groups, teams, departments, specialists, systems and organizations.

Integration is facilitated in three ways. Administration devices integrate the work of specialists. Geographical closeness enables informal integration to take place. Lastly, integration is encouraged by effective downwards direction.

Without effective integration organizations cannot combine their resources to get things done. Cliques develop, defensive walls are erected and massive confusions occur. Everything loses momentum like a slow motion film and labyrinthine procedures proliferate.

Effective integration of effort requires:

Co-ordination | there are appropriate 'mechanisms' for ensuring that integration takes place.
Convenience | potential snarl-ups caused by local geography have been minimized.
Direction | those in the lower levels are told how to play their part in the whole.

Communication for sustaining a healthy community

Organizations are more than collections of inert resources. Emotions, organizational culture, values and principles are all important. They should sustain morale and encourage willingness. This is well understood by great military leaders who carefully nurture 'esprit de corps' in order to have bold and committed armies.

A healthy community is populated by willing people who are generally satisfied, and devote themselves to improvement within the system. The power structure within the organization is accepted. People are valued for their own sake. Closeness and co-operation are present. — Honour

Healthy organizations are detectable by the attitudes that people show. There is obvious care for others. The old-fashioned virtues of fairness, pride in the job and loyalty are present. The word 'goodwill' effectively encapsulates the spirit.

Unhealthy organizations fail to command goodwill. Management are regarded as untrustworthy, the organization is perceived as being unfair or unrewarding, and co-operation is lacking.

Sustaining a healthy community requires:

Honour	people trust management to act with integrity.
Fairness	everyone is treated on the basis of merit and unfair prejudices have been eliminated.
Co-operation	people get together to co-operate on their immediate work tasks and give support to each other.

Communication for making intelligent decisions

You need accurate and speedy information in order to take high quality decisions. This means that important information must be detected and processed quickly. The quality of managerial decisions is partly a function of the effectiveness of the communication system.

Decision making takes place at three levels. First, there are the strategic choices: 'Who are we?', 'How do we sustain our competitiveness?' and 'What are our values?' The decision making at middle level determines how objectives are turned into action programmes. The third level of decision making is practical and concerns how to make the best use of resources to get things done.

Unintelligent decision making is wasteful, hazardous and frustrating and can occur at any of the three levels. The costs of poor decision making are high, sometimes wasting millions,

and often lead industries into bankruptcy or cost countless lives.
   Intelligent decision making requires:

Responsiveness	management (and others with power) get information from below.
Efficiency	red tape has been reduced so that systems are timely and efficient.
Effectiveness	individuals are personally skilled in handling data and communicating effectively.

The next step

These are the four purposes of organizational communication. They provide us with the bare bones of a theory and a reason why we should spend time and money getting communication right. Purposeful communication is an involved topic. Unless we can define what we are talking about there is no possibility of starting any systematic improvement programme. One friend put it this way: 'Until we know what's good, anything is acceptable'. The next chapter elaborates on the theme by enlarging on the twelve components of organizational communication which have been introduced above.

The twelve components of communication

The previous chapter described the four primary purposes of communication. However, looking at the purposes does not tell us how to improve. Advising a man that he should be fit, strong and friendly provides objectives, but not a plan. A useful way of conveying the depth of information needed for planning is to identify the components of organizational communication.

The notion of 'components' needs some explanation. Consider a motor car engine. It has a number of components, each of which must function effectively. Every component – carburettor, pump, flywheel, piston and so on – makes a unique contribution to the performance of the engine. Defective or mistuned components reduce efficiency. A broken component will often cause the motor to fail.

We cannot fix a broken engine until we know what has gone wrong. I recall an incident when a car coughed and spluttered, then broke down. The driver opened the bonnet and gazed at the engine. Clearly he did not know the difference between a spark plug and a big-end. A repair truck was called. The dialogue between the driver and the mechanic was interesting:

> 'It suddenly died on me!'
> 'Is there petrol in the tank?'
> 'Yes, plenty. It's been losing power for an hour or so.'
> 'Describe the problem.'
> 'Well, it sort of jerks when I accelerate.'
> 'I'll look at the electrical system first.'

The mechanic was going through a mental diagnostic checklist to identify symptoms, so that he could direct attention to the most likely source of trouble. This is easier said than done. He must understand the principles of the internal combustion engine and the symptoms of malfunction. Diagnosis is a difficult stage. For example, oil consumption is wildly excessive, but what is the precise cause of the problem? Sometimes a component deteriorates slowly or has an intermittent fault. Perhaps, in the past, some over-enthusiastic fitter has installed a wrong component which can never deliver the correct performance. The most difficult problems occur when several interdependent faults happen at the same time.

Those concerned with overhauling organizational communication should use the same thought process as the garage mechanic. The analogy of an engine with a number of interlinked components working together is helpful for another reason. There is a valid comparison between an engine (which supplies energy to the vehicle) and communication (which is the energizing force of the enterprise).

Once we have a comprehensive diagnostic framework, we can 'lift the bonnet' of the organization with more confidence. The task of detecting malfunctioning components is the first step in repairing and overhauling the system. A defective component is referred to as a 'blockage', because it reduces the efficiency of the system as a whole.

You may have noticed that under each of the four main headings in the previous chapter three additional points were mentioned. These are the twelve key components of organizational communication. They are briefly described below and then expanded at length in the rest of the book.

Communication for sharing the compelling vision

(Finding a viable identity for the organization and ensuring that it is persuasively communicated.)
There are three components:

Sensitivity to the external environment

(Being alert: closely in touch with the world outside.)
Organizations need to communicate with their environment.

This means identifying opportunities, being alert to threats and projecting their image well. Should organizations lose touch with the outside world they become irrelevant. Information from the environment is essential to help organizations keep on track. The overall aim is to create an open system which constantly adapts to changing circumstances. Everyone should keep their eyes and ears open. Top managers study the environment so that the organization can continue to be competitive in tomorrow's world. Further down, managers, specialists and craftsmen must keep up to date with new techniques, ideas and developments.

Communication with the environment is two-way: organizations need to be proactive and influence their environment so that they enjoy the most favourable conditions.

The malfunction of this component causes the blockage 'insensitivity to the external environment'.

Compelling vision

(Being focused: heading for clear goals.)

Senior management must communicate the identity of the organization and define where it is heading. This needs to be expressed as a 'vision of the future' that is seen to be important, coherent and sustainable.

Inspiration, excitement, farsightedness, great clarity and good judgement are necessary ingredients of an inspiring vision of the future. When this does not exist people are inadequately led, aimless and demotivated. The vision is the primary energizing force in the organization.

The compelling vision specifies the strategic driving force of the organization and contains the basic values which determine policies. It may be expressed in words but, most importantly, the vision should be shared by all those who hold positions of power.

The malfunction of this component causes the blockage 'lack of compelling vision'.

Persuasive management

(Being attractive: managers encouraging people to follow.)

Managers must have the communication strategies and skills to encourage people to play a part in transforming the vision into reality. Persuasion forms attitudes, changes behaviour, instils standards and builds a positive climate. Managers should be able to 'sell' the importance of working together for a common cause.

Psychologists have identified distinct techniques for persuasion. These provide guidelines for acquiring true leadership skills. However, persuasion techniques are empty unless they are reinforced by behaviour. Stories, myths and legends are more persuasive than words, and persuasive managements use every device at their disposal.

The malfunction of this component causes the blockage 'unpersuasive management'.

Communication for integrating the effort

(Energy and effort pushing in the same direction.)
There are three components:

Integrating mechanisms

(Being co-ordinated: adequate mechanisms to integrate effort.)
Organizations include specialists, departments and groups. All these must be integrated, so that they work together for the benefit of the organization as a whole. Communication mechanisms need to be devised to enable necessary integration to take place.

The need for integration varies with the size of the organization and the types of work undertaken. Small organizations can be controlled by a single boss, whereas large systems require more elaborate forms of integration. This is made more complex because routine, professional, divisionalized and creative organizations all have different needs. There are distinct mechanisms for integration, ranging from direct supervision to matrix management. Organizations which lack well-developed integrating mechanisms are inefficient, wasteful, incompetent, ponderous, uncreative and fragmented.

The malfunction of this component causes the blockage 'disintegration'.

Helpful geography

(Being convenient: the layout of the organization encourages necessary communication.)

Local geography greatly influences communication patterns. Unfortunately many architects and planners have paid scant attention to the human consequences of their designs. The result is disintegration of both formal and informal communication. The effects of geography on communication extend throughout the organization. Individual work patterns should be helped by the layout of their workplace. Teams should be physically close and relate easily with other teams across boundaries. At the organizational level, divisional and international communication problems are commonplace. Careful consideration at the building design stage and intelligent use of electronic media can reduce communication blockages caused by geographical inconvenience.

The malfunction of this component causes the blockage 'unhelpful geography'.

Downward flow

(Being directive: people are told what they should know to play their part.)

All sizeable organizations are hierarchical and power is centralised at the top. This means that only those with seniority can see the whole picture. Objectives, policies, procedures, disciplines, success measures, controls and directives all need to be reliably cascaded down. This is an essential integrating force.

Downward communication enables organizations to be controlled by action planning, performance control or the enforcement of company policies. The flow of information downwards is by one of these four methods: down the line, through representatives of the workforce, by methods of mass communication or using techniques of training and indoctrination.

The malfunction of this component causes the blockage 'defective downward flow'.

Communication for sustaining a healthy community

(People working for the organization, not against it.)
There are three components:

High trust

(Being honourable: people trust those with power.)
Trust means people knowing they can rely on each other. When there is insufficient trust communication suffers badly; what is said is not believed. Trust is vital for sustaining a healthy community by stimulating constructive relationships and encouraging goodwill. Self-interest, if carried to extremes, is destructive to organizations. However, trust cannot be manufactured by deception; managers will only be trusted if they behave in trustworthy ways.

Trust is based on managers being honest, consistent, realistic, following-through and acting fairly and decently. Trust is a personal decision. It is built when leaders behave with integrity and principle. Once destroyed, trust can only be rebuilt with painful slowness.

The malfunction of this component causes the blockage 'low trust'.

Lack of prejudice

(Being fair: no categories of people are disadvantaged.)
People are disposed to treat various groups as inferiors. Such prejudiced attitudes cause major communication problems. Healthy communities are based on the principle of fairness. The most common kinds of prejudice are racial, sexual, religious and between social classes.

Prejudice is destructive because it increases social distance and decreases humanness. This is particularly damaging because prejudice is often energized by aggression and hostility. Disadvantaged groups, once they begin to organize and protest, present major problems for managers. Energy is swallowed up by conflict. Unfairness undermines a sense of unity.

In particular, organizations which are fragmented by social class differences have major difficulties. Groups take traditional roles and owe allegiance to their class rather than to the whole organization.

The malfunction of this component causes the blockage 'prejudice'.

Supportive teamwork

(Being co-operative: people work well together.)

Teamwork, in all its forms, is essential in healthy communities because it gives people a sense of personal worth and provides the support needed to share ideas, agree objectives, develop plans and use others' strengths.

Supportive teamwork requires respect for difference. People play distinct roles in teams. All the different contributions need to be co-ordinated by a skilled process manager who builds an effective team from a disparate group of individuals.

Teams must also avoid being riddled by destructive games. Negative relationships destroy teamwork by undermining the quality of human support and generating defensiveness.

The malfunction of this component causes the blockage 'unsupportive teamwork'.

Communication for making intelligent decisions

(Efficiently collecting, structuring and transmitting relevant information to those with power.)

There are three components:

Upward flow

(Being responsive: encouraging data to flow upwards so that managers know what is going on.)

Managers need to receive communication from below. This means being in touch with all employees. Intelligence must be gathered so that potential problems and opportunities are well understood. Creative ideas often come from below.

Managers need to gather data from below for five reasons: to collect information about strengths, weaknesses, opportunities and threats; to harvest ideas and creativity; to take the temperature of the organization; to be open to challenge and to be seen to be responsive.

There are three principal methods of gathering data from below: by channelling information upwards through the management hierarchy; by direct contact between senior managers and people on the shopfloor and through surveys. Information from the internal environment is essential for wise decision making.

The malfunction of this component causes the blockage 'defective upward flow'.

Apt administration

(Being efficient: not having excessively cumbersome and costly channels for communication.)

Channels of decision making and communication can become slow and inefficient; much unnecessary communication can take place. Tortuous and wasteful communication is 'red tape'; it consumes much time and generates frustration. Red tape needs to be fought and defeated but, like the weeds in a garden, it easily grows again!

Different types of organizations have their own kinds of red tape. Simple organizations, reporting to one boss, rarely have elaborate systems. However, large organizations which may be ruled by procedures can become encumbered by stultifying disciplines. Those organizations which give a professional service become disintegrated and difficult to manage as a whole. Many large organizations have broken into separate divisions as an antidote to excessive red tape. However, red tape is most destructive in those creative organizations which are trying to push back the frontiers of knowledge or technology.

The malfunction of this component causes the blockage 'inapt administration'.

Communication skills

(Being effective: people have the ability to communicate well.)

Individual communication skills, both spoken and written, are the foundation of effective organizational communication. Individuals must be able to express themselves effectively otherwise mistakes occur, opportunities are missed, and poor decisions are taken.

Communication skills include: accurate self-perception, assertion, active listening, leadership, methodical approaches to problem solving and decision making, counselling, dealing with unconstructive people, trainer competence, creativity, writing skills and oral communication competence.

The malfunction of this component causes the blockage 'inadequate communication skills'.

Purposeful organizational communication

We can now define purposeful organizational communication with precision. It exists when all twelve components are functioning well. Read the definition below and consider how your own organization compares. Only when all twelve conditions are met should you throw this book in the waste paper basket and rest content.

Purposeful organizational communication means that:

- people at all levels are sensitive to changes in the outside environment
- top managers give inspiration and direction
- managers are skilful persuaders
- the work of specialists is well integrated
- all possible steps are taken to overcome geographical barriers
- everyone knows what is required of them
- those with power are trusted
- no group is treated as inferior because of prejudice
- people support each other in teams
- there is an effective flow of 'bottom-up' communication
- communication processes are speedy and cost-effective
- individuals are skilled in personal communication.

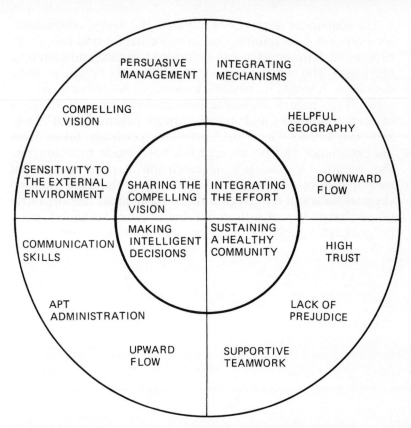

The twelve components of organizational communication

So that's it. Four main purposes of organizational communication, each having three components. All are equally important and must be actively pursued at the same time. Managers need to be skilful jugglers with twelve balls in the air. The diagram summarizes the position.

The remainder of this book explores the twelve components for purposeful communication in more depth, and begins the process of defining what can be done to reduce and eliminate blockages. The twelve component chapters are not meant to be definitive. It would be possible to write an entire book on each topic! Rather, each chapter draws out the distinctive character of each component and suggests where organizational blockages can occur. The illustrations are generally taken from my experience and no attempt has been made to summarize the wealth of academic research on various aspects of communication. At the end of each chapter there are practical suggestions about how to go further. Remember that organizational change begins with insight but requires sustained action programmes to unblock organizational communication.

Sharing the compelling vision

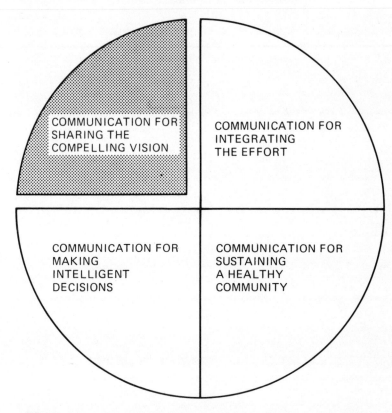

'Finding a viable identity for the organization and ensuring that it is persuasively communicated.'

Definitions

Share – 'in common with others'

Compel – 'to urge irresistibly'

Vision – 'a mental concept of a distinct and vivid kind; a highly imaginative scheme or anticipation'

Shorter Oxford Dictionary

Sensitivity to the external environment

Being alert: closely in touch with the world outside.

The business school was an imposing building set in well-manicured lawns. A group of chief executives had come for a two-week course on 'Contemporary Business Strategy'. They sat in a lecture theatre, looking like overgrown schoolchildren, and listened to a presentation on 'The role of top management'. Their professor, a slight and wiry man who danced with nervous energy, expounded: 'I emphasize that your businesses can only survive if you have a sustainable competitive advantage. You have to really *know* your competition and really *know* your markets. You must study your environment with the care that a new mother gives to her child. Outstanding companies must discover exactly what the market wants; then they act on what they find. They supply tomorrow's needs, not yesterday's.'

This professor was talking about an aspect of communication: the extent to which organizations are in touch with their environments. Many organizations have suffered the serious consequences of insensitivity to the external environment. Examples include a police force facing an unpredicted race riot and US soldiers overrun by Indians at the Little Big Horn. The Polish army at the start of World War II gave a tragic illustration. A Polish general ordered a cavalry charge against Nazi tanks. The resulting deaths demonstrated the appalling consequences of using redundant ideas. There are numerous other illustrations of the point. British motorcycle manufacturers and the Swiss watch industry both ignored the importance of new technology. Organizations which fail to keep in touch with their environment become obsolescent and perish.

The lesson is simple: no organization is an island. The environment is always in flux, but in the late twentieth century the pace of change is unusually rapid. There are few oases of stability left in the world. Organizations must have their eyes and ears open, and establish a flow of communication with the environment to detect market opportunities, enable threats to be identified and provide the stimulus to keep up to date.

The requirement to communicate with the environment affects people at each hierarchical level. Everyone needs to keep open. Top managers are concerned with broad technological, social, economic and political factors, whilst the more junior managers, specialists and craftsmen keep in touch with new ideas and techniques which are relevant to their own specialisms.

In this chapter we examine sensitivity to the environment from four perspectives. First, we consider the organization as a living entity which needs to adapt constantly to a changing world. The role of the 'brain of the firm' is our second focus. Every person needs to detect changes in the environment and this provides the third perspective. Lastly, we reverse the analysis and examine how organizations can be proactive in influencing their own environments.

Organizations as living entities

All living organisms have some capacity to adapt to a changing environment, and need suitable antennae to sense the world outside. Organizations in a changing world must interact with their environment at many levels and become 'open systems'. (For a further discussion of this concept see D. Katz and R. Kahn, *The Social Psychology of Organizations*, John Wiley and Sons Inc., New York 1978.)

The concept of an open system is somewhat abstract but has great relevance. There are six particularly important ideas:

1   An open system takes energy from the environment and undergoes continuous replenishment.

2   A closed system fails to recharge itself and runs down.
3   Open systems obtain feedback from their environment to
     help them keep on track.
4   Open systems constantly adjust the way they work to
     maintain poise and effectiveness.
5   Larger systems become more specialized, so management
     must have a strategy to collect and process complex
     information.
6   'There are many ways of killing the cat' – the manager in
     open system is more concerned with the question: 'What
     will work?' than the question: 'What is the traditional way?'

Evidence suggests that open systems survive and closed systems
perish as they lose touch with the world outside. Organizational
sociologists have a jargon of their own, describing open system
concepts in terms of boundaries, entropy, feedback loops,
dynamic homeostatus, differentiation, and equifinality. Managers may find such terms 'turn them off', but open systems
concepts are worth struggling with. They help us to understand
the reasons why effective communication with the outside world
is so important.

An example from military history shows how much resource
may have to be put into maintaining an open system. In World
War II, the propaganda effort directed against Nazi Germany
was co-ordinated by the Political Warfare Executive in England. They collected German newspapers, carefully monitored
radio programmes, conducted lengthy interviews with prisoners
and took every opportunity to understand the moods and
conditions of the enemy. In 1944 more than half a million
documents were received, read and filed to help the propagandists assess public opinion in Axis Europe. This German material
was sorted into eight main groups, and then broken down into
numerous subgroups. For example, the topic of 'internal
politics' was broken down into sections like faith in Hitler,
attitude to the Gestapo, loyalty to the régime and so on. The
propagandists knew the people they addressed intimately so
that not a single false note crept into their propaganda.

Japanese industrialists, who are today's masters of business
strategy, make no secret of the fact that they keep their
organizational systems open by collecting huge amounts of data

on their markets with the same care as the British Political Warfare Executive. In Japanese boardrooms they talk of 'taking the customer's skin temperature daily'. Such companies truly create a culture of vigilance.

An organization must be open to more than its customers. For example, national cultural factors are most important. Environments differ from nation to nation. When Honda first went to California to sell motorcycles they used the selling point that the handlebars 'are shaped like the eyebrows of Buddha'; it went well in Japan, but it was nonsense in California. But they were open to the environment, changed their approach, and sold a great many motorcycles.

The brain of the firm

Top managers are the only group who can direct the organization. In a real sense they are 'the brain of the firm'. Failure to perform this function means that the organization drifts, loses a sense of purpose and misses key opportunities. Top managers make fundamental decisions about the direction and the identity of the enterprise.

This is easy to assert but is much more difficult in practice. Perhaps the most significant problem for top managers is handling complexity. So much data on the environment are available that managers can be swallowed by a quicksand of information. Important factors are hidden in a surfeit of data. There are two remedies, both of which are indispensable.

First, top managers must use the principles of scientific method to structure the data they collect. Generations of scientists have learned how to cope with hugely complex phenomena and understand the essences of things. The principles of scientific method – objectivity, structured observation, hypothesis, experimentation and research – are the only proven way of making sense of a vastly complex world.

Secondly, even with the most sophisticated rational systems, top managers must use their experience, instincts and hunches. Some matters are too ephemeral or unpredictable for intellectual analysis. We must trust the wisdom and judgement of shrewd people. Despite all the disadvantages of relying on individual insight there is no alternative; some people have the capacity to 'feel' what is right.

Henry Mintzberg has been an inspiration to me on this topic. He gives an excellent example of the need for a synthesis between head and heart as he describes how Sam Steinberg, a Canadian retailing entrepreneur, chose to see changes in the environment as a crisis rather than a problem. This forced his managers to act. Sam Steinberg realized the importance of understanding the environment when he said: 'Nobody knew the grocery business like we did. Everything has to do with your knowledge. I knew merchandise, I knew cost, I knew selling, I knew customers, I knew everything...and I passed on all my knowledge; I kept teaching my people. That's the advantage we had. They couldn't touch it.'

The essence of Steinberg's genius was the ability to be in touch with basics; not so busy with big issues that he got trapped in the corporate stratosphere. His rational and intuitive understanding of the environment enabled him to pick out the discontinuities, signs that patterns were changing. He was willing to live with uncertainty, to step into void, and throw aside preconceptions. Steinberg's willingness to make fundamental changes was demonstrated when he boasted to a newspaper reporter that 'not a cent of money outside the family is invested in the company' and a few months later announced that the company would go to the capital market to finance a massive five-year expansion programme. How did Steinberg see that a revolution in retailing was needed? The answer lies in the character of the man. Communication with the environment can never be purely rational. Latent or emerging needs must be seen before they become commonplace. (See H. Mintzberg, 'The Mind of the Strategist(s)' in *The Executive Mind* by Suresch Srivastva and Associates, Jossey-Boss Publishers, San Francisco 1983.)

Steinberg showed that the brain of the firm must be capable of an intellectual leap to predict changes in the environment. This is made difficult, as readers of spy stories will know, because the enemy will seek to confuse. For example, a new competitor enters your market with lower prices. Are they more efficient, or are they trying to squeeze you out while bearing a short-term loss? You don't know. Market intelligence and competitor analysis may give some insight, but the competitor is 'muddying the water' so as to confuse competition. Top management must act on hunch.

Being close to the environment increases the probability that a viable vision of the future will be chosen for your organization. This requires choosing a mission that is achievable, desirable and sustainable in a competitive environment. In the next chapter we will examine these matters in more depth, but it is important to realize that the environment is the examination room in which the strategic decisions of top management are put to the test.

Perceptive leaders do all they can to keep open to the 'feel of the market'. There is no substitute for personal contact. The chairman of Oberoi Hotels, perhaps the East's finest hotel chain, personally reads the comments left by guests. Directors of the BBC regularly meet viewers and listeners to discuss their viewpoints. Managers must design systems for keeping sensitive to their particular environment and have the self-discipline to leave the tidy order of the executive office and go out into the world of real people.

Such intimate knowledge of the external environment provides the intelligence for assertive management. An example makes the point. Marks and Spencer suffered a £55 million decline in its share of the British clothing industry in 1985. The company realized the problem was that they could not respond quickly enough to changes in the market. The solution was to institute a more flexible marketing policy with shorter production runs, maximizing the strength of local sourcing to shorten order and reorder lead times, so allowing a much faster response to actual sales trends.

Not all top teams are concerned with profit, but it can be argued that communication with the environment probably occurs more easily in commercial than in non-commercial organizations. After all, a business will see its livelihood disappear if it persists in being environmentally blind. One of the most impressive achievements of the capitalist system is to require organizations to keep in touch with their environment through the tyranny of the profit and loss account. Non-commercial organizations suffer dire consequences more slowly and can remain more comfortably out of touch.

When top teams function as the brain of the firm they keep in constant touch with the environment and can thus ensure the following conditions:

1 A clear statement of markets served and precise identification of who their customers are.
2 An explicit understanding of what existing customers want today.
3 Sound predictions of what their customers are likely to want in the future.
4 A recognition of who their competitors are, their strengths, weaknesses and strategies.
5 Careful evaluation of future opportunities, possible benefits and risks.
6 Understanding of the social, economic and political factors which influence the market.
7 An objective recognition of corporate strengths and weaknesses.

Just as the cortex of the brain has specialized areas – one for sight, one for hearing and so on – so does a top team. Perhaps the most significant change in management since 1960 is the rise in power of an aggressive enfant terrible – marketing. There are few large companies who do not have a vice-president or director of marketing, who is specifically responsible for keeping track of the outside world. The marketing function communicates with the environment from a position of power. Today, marketeers are close to the heart of organizational government, performing an essential service in lifting the corporate gaze away from the corporate navel.

As marketeers will never tire of telling you, their functional commitment is not enough. The entire corporation needs to be attuned to the marketplace. They are right, but you must struggle to provide something with intrinsic value in tomorrow's marketplace. If Stravinsky had written for the market of his day we would have had more Viennese waltzes, and no 'Rite of Spring'.

Individual adaptation

It is not only top teams which must communicate with the

environment. Individuals need to be responsive. It is almost impossible to think of a job which is not changing through new technology or revised systems – apart from a masseur in a Turkish bath and practitioners of the world's oldest profession. New skills, techniques and concepts are ignored at your peril.

Most roles have a job description which lays down the purpose, duties, authority and responsibility of the job holder. This may be supplemented by a specification of the knowledge and skills. But job descriptions are a snapshot in time. It is dangerous to think of a job like a mammoth frozen into a block of Siberian ice. Many organizations find it is useful to identify the expected rate of change for each job and then what action should be taken to prepare individuals for the future. Manufacturers write in their brochures: 'Our policy is to improve continuously the quantity and quality of our product and so the specifications may vary from those described'. People working at all levels must learn to adopt the same philosophy to their own lives or run the risk of personal obsolescence.

In fact, all creatures must keep open to the environment. Students of the common rabbit report that the latrine areas are 'computer banks' of important, regularly updated information. A perceptive rabbit, when sniffing around the warren's latrine, will learn much about the current physical and sexual wellbeing of the neighbourhood rabbits. Such information, gained through diagnostic sniffs at rabbit droppings, enables young male rabbits to set their priorities for the day.

Keeping up to date requires you to become sensitive to ways in which changes in the outside world are likely to affect you. Without this information people continue to behave in their customary ways. A psychologist friend, Dr Barry Goodfield, puts it this way: 'Practice does not make perfect but permanent. We are not passive cat's paws who are the playthings of the outside world. People have the capacity to influence their own lives if they maintain competencies relevant to tomorrow's world.' Individuals need to study the factors which may influence their careers in the future. (See Dave Francis, *Managing Your Own Career*, Collins, London 1985.)

Narrowing the focus to the job level, the following questions may help you to become more sensitive to the effects of change:

1   Who are the best people doing this job at the present time?
2   What are they doing that I am not doing?
3   How is new technology likely to affect my current job over the next three years?
4   How are new concepts of effectiveness likely to affect my job over the next three years?
5   What are the possible ways in which my current job will be undertaken in ten years from now?
6   Is the extent of likely change radical or insignificant?
7   What is the probability that I will acquire the required new knowledge and skills if my present trend of learning continues?
8   Does the organization possess effective training and development programmes?
9   What initiatives can I take to help myself?

People require encouragement to look outwards. A programme to heighten awareness of the environment is often required. I was once a consultant to the purchasing department of an electronics factory. Their methods were traditional. Boxes of well-thumbed cards filled a large office where the clerks sat surrounded by mounds of paperwork. It was a scene reminiscent of a black and white movie of the 1950s. Their manager decided to computerize, but the supervisors and clerks were totally preoccupied with feeding the existing systems and felt too overworked to consider the new ideas. As the manager said: 'We are all blinkered. The world outside has changed and we haven't.'

An action learning programme to increase the department's environmental sensitivity was begun. Films were hired, lecturers invited in, and the members of the department were sent by bus to be shown up-to-date buying systems in other factories. The department members began to see their own systems as old-fashioned, and they developed a vision of the changes needed for themselves. Computerization was installed with great enthusiasm and success. The members of the purchasing department went outside their limited environment and realized, for themselves, that they had to change.

To summarize, there are five ways to increase individual responsiveness to the environment:

1   Change the people concerned (sometimes old dogs won't learn new tricks).
2   Spell out the changes needed and counsel people about what they should do.
3   Create experiences for people which demonstrate that their present recipes are inadequate (like the purchasing department described above).
4   Broaden individuals' experiences through lateral movement.
5   Undertake a programme of cultural changes to create new norms and behaviours.

Influencing the environment

So far we have discussed why top management and people throughout organizations need to look outwards. However, the traffic is not all one way; organizations need to influence their environment. Obvious ways include advertising and public relations, but there are many subtle methods to affect attitudes. Colin Marshall, as president of Avis, was well aware of this when he said in a television interview: 'The girls and men on the retail counters portray the image of the company – so top management has to make sure that the image is right.' Every public action is a form of communication.

Some wise organizations have begun to spend a lot of time on trying to influence the political and social environment in which they operate. For example, in a private memorandum to his senior staff, the chief executive of one international corporation said: 'We will track all the significant political parties, get to know local and national politicians and build good relationships with them, and follow the same approach with the press, other media and anyone who may be able to help us from the government services. All executives will become skilled in putting up a good public front, either to the local community or for the media.'

Some of the clearest illustrations of proactive communication with the environment come from tobacco companies. More than twenty years ago it became clear that tobacco products were major health hazards, yet the clever manipulations of advertising budgets has blunted the impact of the stark medical facts. Brands of cigarettes are associated with exciting sporting events, the vigour of the cowboy and prestigious lifestyles. Packaging is subtly designed by psychological experts so that the product is perceived to be valuable and innocuous. Vast sums have been spent on lobbying governments to take a benign stance to smokers. These tactics have paid off. People still smoke in their millions, which they would not do if cigarettes were advertised by a terminally ill bronchitic and sold in a brown paper bag labelled 'cancer and halitosis sticks'.

Those organizations which are actively trying to influence their environment are likely to be:

1 Very clear what their present image is.
2 Very clear about how they wish to be seen.
3 Taking active steps to 'make friends' where it counts.
4 Using expert advice to tune their public image.
5 Training key executives in projecting themselves to the media.
6 Reviewing the image created by the output from the organization.

Organizations must do whatever they can to make their environment more hospitable. In a hostile and competitive world every organism needs to be alert to threat and perceive opportunity. As Darwin explained, 'survival requires adaptation'. And adaptation requires environmental sensitivity. If Darwin's maxim is forgotten, then dire consequences follow.

Is insensitivity to the external environment a blockage in your organization?

The following activities from the companion volume, *50 Activities for Unblocking Organizational Communication*, are especially relevant:

1 Customer feedback.
2 Understanding your environment.
3 Strategic intelligence.

Compelling vision
Being focused: heading for clear goals.

One day I was sitting in my office when the telephone rang and I heard the familiar West Coast accent of Barry Goodfield, my larger-than-life psychologist friend. Barry was calling from Amsterdam and his voice was electric with excitement. He said: 'Would you like to join me and some friends for a weekend in three weeks time? I've chartered a sailing clipper called *De Hoop* and we will spend the weekend sailing, drinking Geneva gin, having wonderful conversations and swimming. We'll sail down to Enkhuizen, which is a magic Dutch port, and you'll be eating soused herring from a pavement stall. I have reserved a victorian admiral's sailing cap for you. I really want you to join us.'

I listened to Barry and felt myself growing keener by the moment. Three weeks later, on the KLM flight to Amsterdam, I reflected on how I had decided to join the party. During the telephone conversation Barry painted a desirable image of the future which had a place for me. As he spoke, I saw in my mind's eye, an old sailing clipper dashing, full sailed, across a sun-sparkling sea. I wanted to be part of that weekend, both to contribute and enjoy.

Barry was acting as a true leader when he communicated that compelling vision which captured my commitment. The imaginative term 'compelling vision' was coined by Warren Bennis (see W. Bennis and B. Nanus, *Leaders*, Harper & Row, New York 1985), and is a vital ingredient of leadership behaviour.

Those who are outstandingly successful as managers, army generals, teachers or parents, are able to articulate a vivid description – or vision – of the future and then convince others to help make this vision become a reality.

The concept of a 'vision of the future' is an invaluable tool. Without a corporate vision an organization becomes unsteerable and drifts hopelessly, like a ship without a rudder. The clear communication of a valid and achievable vision is the most important task of senior management.

A compelling vision is a tapestry woven from several different strands. The important threads have been known since before Hannibal persuaded doubtful elephant drivers to take their beasts over the Swiss Alps. A compelling vision must capture people's imaginations, yet be achievable. The end results must be felt to be worthwhile.

Each individual has to gain and contribute. Wise generals and managers set their compelling vision to stretch, but not overwhelm, the competence of their organization. Oliver Cromwell clearly understood the motivational power of a compelling vision when he insisted that his forces must 'know what they fight for and love what they know'.

A compelling vision may be a single brilliant thought which captivates the world, or a thoroughly researched concept which develops only after a painstaking evaluation of options. Open, honest and skilful top teamwork provides the human mechanism to devise a realistic but exciting vision.

A vision of the future is the foundation of strategy. Generals, when not at war, spend much of their time planning how they would respond to a military crisis. They develop scenarios and simulate conflicts on huge computer war games. We can learn from the clear distinction which army generals make between strategy and tactics. The question the strategist asks is 'What do we want to achieve?' whereas the tactical specialist asks a very different question: 'How can we achieve?'

Sources of visions

Now a somewhat complex but important idea. Visions of the

future come from two sources: either inspired from the wider environment or from deep within the person.

Visions inspired by the wider environment are 'world-driven'. The visionary gets in touch with an external meaning or need and responds to this. Implicit in world-driven visions is the idea that the world should be served. Such needs may be economic (serving wealth), spiritual (serving God), environmental (serving the physical world), intellectual (serving knowledge), artistic (serving beauty), communal (serving man) and so on.

Visions inspired from within the individual are 'self-driven'. The visionary gets in touch with a meaning or need from deep within, and allows this to grow. Implicit in self-driven visions is the idea that the world is fertile ground for man to express himself. Such expressions of individuality may be commercial (making money), hedonistic (seeking pleasure), power-oriented (making a mark), acquisitive (amassing things), and so on.

The formative process is different for world-driven and self-driven visions. World-driven visions are derived from outer imperatives which compel or attract the individual, whereas self-driven visions are energized from within.

World-driven	*Self-driven*
Be open to the world	Look inside yourself
Allow messages to enter	Decide what you want to do
Feel the importance that emerges	Find ways for self-expression
Pick the most promising strategy	Find your vocation
Set objectives and plans	Go through trials and tribulations
Do what serves you best	Do what you have to do

A vision of the future is much more than a soulless plan. It has spirit, will and energy. The internal processes needed for visioning and planning are quite distinct:

Planning	*Visioning*
(Theme: sense)	(Theme: desire)
Rational analysis	Emotional
Computer models	Individualistic

Systems-based	Inspired
Bureaucratic	Simple
Long time frame	Enduring
Logically defensible	Committed
Complex	Single-minded
Factual	Bold
Scenarios	Ruthless
Risk assessment	Compelling
Disciplined	Organic

Visioning is the fundamental step. As we discussed in the previous chapter, visions then need to be validated in the external environment to see whether they are conceivable and desirable. The dialogue between visioning and validation is the essence of strategy.

Choosing a compelling vision

The compelling vision for an organization has two interconnected components. First, it must identify what the organization is devoted to doing well, that is, specify its strategic driving force. Secondly, it must identify the beliefs and core values which give the organization its identity as a productive community.

In extending and updating the pioneer work of Tregoe and Zimmerman (B. Tregoe and J. Zimmerman, *Top Management Strategy*, John Martin Publishing, London 1980) it is useful to define the strategic driving forces of organizations. The need was put succinctly by a manager friend who said: 'Managements need to identify their core business and devote their attention solely to the field that they know well. Dissipation of effort is a common cause of weakness. This means being simple, clear, focused and single-minded.'

There are twelve possible strategic driving forces. Each organization (or unit) should know exactly what its strategic driving force is, and what it is not. Organizations become confused and unfocused when they try to follow several strategic driving forces at once.

37

Twelve strategic driving forces

1 'State-of-the-art'

This organization is devoted to being a leader in its chosen field. The state-of-the-art organization generates business by doing things in more advanced or clever ways than anyone else. The organization is a powerhouse of creativity and is constantly changing as new technology develops. Innovation is highly prized. Only the most modern will do. Customers are attracted by getting the best or newest goods or services.

The state-of-the-art organization invests in highly qualified people, advanced facilities, education, training, experimenting, and giving freedom to people (examples: design laboratories, experimental treatment hospitals, research-based consultancies).

2 'Professional service'

This organization provides its customers with highly skilled individual services. The professional service organization enables qualified individuals to carry out their specialized tasks. The principles and skills are guarded by professional bodies (like the British Medical Association or the American Bar Association). Customers are attracted to professional service organizations because they have complex human needs which need to be met. Such organizations tend to be responsible and traditional, gradually evolving with scientific or social development.

The professional service organization invests in qualified people, providing them with support and resources to do their work. There is much emphasis on training and standards of behaviour (examples: most hospitals, schools, social work agencies etc.).

3 'Product producer'

This organization is devoted to producing goods or services and offering them to defined markets. Product producer organizations have product ranges which are not tailormade for individual customers. Customers are attracted by products which are desirable and good value for money.

The product producer organization invests in market specification and research, product design, manufacturing, limited research and development, distribution and selling. It concentrates on developing within its chosen range of products and extending their attractiveness and market scope (examples: mass production motor manufacturers, pharmaceutical companies, book publishers).

4 'Experience provider'

This organization provides people with experiences which they enjoy or value. The experience provider organization generates business by meeting a human need for sensation, stimulation or edification.

The experience provider organization aims to understand totally and fulfil a need or want. This may be for entertainment (a theatre), for excitement (an action holiday), for fantasy (a strip club), for interest (a museum), for spiritual experience (a church), or any human needs. Such organizations concentrate on the depth and breadth of the receiver's experience. The experience provider organization invests in careful market research, novelty, continued enhancement of facilities and a fashionable image (examples: Kissograms, Disneyland and other theme parks, St. Paul's Cathedral and most other spiritual centres).

5 'Market server'

This organization fulfils all the needs of a defined market. There are many markets and market segments like fishermen, electrical contractors, stamp collectors or secretaries. Customers are attracted to the market server organization because it can meet most or all of their needs.

The market server organization invests in breadth of provision of goods and services. It is very conscious of its particular market segment and works hard to maintain a good relationship with its customers. It is alert to new needs and constantly tries to predict what its customers will require (examples: electrical wholesalers, fishing shops, mother-to-be retailers).

6 'System provider'

This organization enables other organizations to communicate or co-ordinate. The system provider organization generates business by enabling complex operations to be performed. Such systems may be electronic, logistical or managerial; the essence is providing a capability to others which enables them to manage complexity.

The system provider organization invests in identifying needs for communication or co-ordination and developing both hardware and software to provide a wide range of systems. System reliability, cost effectiveness, and system integrity are key. Such organizations are constantly extending the scope of their systems and their capabilities (examples: electronic messaging, telephone companies, data processing companies).

7 'Production contractor'

This organization provides a facility for others to get things built, constructed, repaired, adapted or manufactured. The production contractor organization generates business by enabling specialist tasks to be done for those without the will or resources to do the work themselves. The essence of their business is that they contract to supply specific services which maintain or add value to products.

The production contractor organization invests in equipment, systems and facilities to do the kind of work that it specializes in. This may be workshop facilities, production systems, skilled human resources etc. (examples: food packers, television studios, servicing garages).

8 'Profit cow'

This organization makes money for its owners. It is solely a resource for making profit and is exploited only so long as it is the best way of using the capital tied up in ownership. All managerial decisions are taken with the intention of maximizing profitability. The profit cow organization generates business by providing channels to exploit the commercial acumen of its owners.

The profit cow organization invests only in high-return prospects, and has no loyalty to any industry, activity, country or people (examples: freelance entrepreneurs, asset stripping organizations).

9 'Resource ownership'

This organization acquires valuable resources and exploits them. There are two types of resource ownership enterprises. The first owns land, space, minerals, raw materials, crops, animals, or things cultivated and grown. This type generates business because it possesses and distributes commodities which others need and want. The second type of resource ownership is the large conglomerate which acquires a portfolio of companies that are measured on their performance. The portfolio is treated as an estate and adapted to maximize profitability over the medium and long term.

The resource ownership organization invests in expanding its portfolio of investments and harvesting what it owns. It seeks to extend its ownership to new resources. Research is done into the best ways of exploiting resources. Long-time horizons may be required (examples: oil companies, large conglomerates, forestry owners).

10 'Distribution capability'

This organization moves physical products to where they are needed. This may be by air, rail, sea, road, canal, space flight, mail etc. The distribution capability organization generates business by providing systems and vehicles for efficient transportation of tangible items without damaging them. It exploits its distribution capability in as many ways as possible.

The distribution capability organization invests in systems, facilities, comprehensive coverage, planning, specialized vehicles, co-ordination and communication, and start-to-finish service (examples: international messenger services, frozen food distributors).

11 'Maintenance of order'

This organization maintains order. It protects property and services, people, peace, and the rights of the citizen. The maintenance of order organization generates business by enabling other activities to proceed unhindered. There are two types. The first is concerned with security. On the national scale the armed forces have this role, whereas local police, courts, security guards etc. perform similar functions at the community level. The second type provides services like cleaning, repairing, painting, maintaining, monitoring, inspecting and surveying.

The maintenance of order organization invests in predicting threats and having the capability to meet them. This includes the use of force, special expertise, trained manpower, dedicated equipment, fast response times and communication and control structures etc. (examples: security firms, waste disposal, the police).

12 'Self-expression'

This organization provides facilities for members to do what they need or want to do. Satisfaction includes enjoyment, self-expression, enlightenment, comradeship, support, stimulation etc. The self-expression organization sustains itself because people wish to contribute and give voluntarily. Such organizations are frequently non-commercial.

The self-expression organization invests in its membership and facilities. Resources are allocated to create conditions in which people can 'do their own thing' (examples: amateur theatre, associations of teachers of management, old people's day centres).

Developing a compelling vision

These twelve strategic driving forces provide the basis of a viable compelling vision which becomes the single driving force of the organization. The viability of the choice is partly determined by the environment – that is why the analysis in the chapter on 'Sensitivity to the external environment' is so important. Once determined, *all* aspects of the organization should be shaped to actualize the driving force.

A compelling vision is especially necessary in non-commercial organizations. The recent history of one urban library service gives an excellent example. It became apparent that the library was providing a white middle-class service, despite population changes which meant that the local community had become multiracial. Senior librarians developed a new compelling vision of their role which they defined as 'to meet the real needs of the present community'. Libraries were changed to become more accessible, book-buying policy was radically altered and action taken to attract a multi-ethnic readership. The senior librarians had been alerted to the need for a new compelling vision by local politicians who were in daily contact with a wide cross-section of the community.

For all organizations, an effective compelling vision has these key characteristics:

1   The compelling vision is based on a discerning analysis of the present situation and the capability of the organization.
2   Options have been well evaluated.
3   The chosen vision appeals to basic desires of members of the organization.
4   The output of the organization is either needed or wanted by customers.
5   The compelling vision identifies the single strategic driving force of the organization.
6   The future is seen to have the possibility of real achievement. Individual organization members should be able to bathe in the reflected glory of success.
7   The compelling vision is felt to be achievable although it will stretch people.
8   From time to time the compelling vision is re-evaluated and either changed or reaffirmed.

Not all visions of the future are constructive. Some appear attractive at first sight but turn out to be false, shallow or unworkable. For example, in the 1950s many architects' dreams of a leap forward in urban design were absurdly Utopian and based on false assumptions. Their egotistic dreams became a nightmare for those forced to live in the concrete monstrosities they created. The lesson is that visions need to be validated before they are implemented. This is done by:

○ devising an effective rational planning system to validate ideas (checks and balances in decision making)
○ following the lessons of history (there is much collected wisdom in tradition)
○ consulting widely (listen to divergent viewpoints)
○ working from a well-developed body of principles (ensure depth)
○ experimenting before full commitment (test ideas)
○ being willing to live with the results (self testing).

The word which top managers frequently use to describe their vision of the future is 'mission'. The root is 'mittere', the Latin verb meaning 'to send'. A missionary goes forth to preach the faith. A corporate mission is the compelling vision of the organization which has been sent to inspire and guide people.

Powerful mission statements are based on deeper values than mere profitability and commercial advantage. Organizations which are consistently high performers have leaders who pay explicit attention to values and want to feel a lasting sense of pride in what they create. Leaders know that their primary role is to breathe meaning into the mission of the organization. Winston Churchill, President J.F. Kennedy and Martin Luther King showed us the attracting power of a mission based on deeply held values.

The importance of incorporating beliefs and values into a vision of the corporate future has been well understood by leading Japanese industrialists. One Japanese businessman clearly laid down the gauntlet when he made the following remarks to a group of Western managers:

> Only by drawing on the combined brain power of all its employees can a firm face up to the turbulence and constraints of today's environment.
>
> This is why our large companies give their employees three to four times more training than yours, this is why they foster within the firm such intensive exchange and communication; this is why they seek constantly every-

body's suggestions and why they demand from the educational system increasing numbers of graduates as well as bright and well-educated generalists, because these people are the lifeblood of industry.

Your 'socially minded bosses', often full of good intentions, believe their duty is to protect the people in their firms. We, on the other hand, are realists and consider it our duty to get our own people to defend their firms which will pay them back a hundredfold for their dedication. By doing this, we end up by being more 'social' than you.

In general, useful mission statements:

1 State the strategic driving force of the organization.
2 Say what the organization is not.
3 Are cautiously optimistic (realistic and believable).
4 Arise from deeds and personal beliefs, not wishful hopes.
5 Avoid high-sounding and pious wording.
6 Are lucid and readily understandable.
7 Show benefit to customers, employees and owners.
8 Respect the distinguished history of the organization.
9 Include values towards customers, employees, managers, communities and shareholders.
10 Answer the question: 'Why would we be proud to work for this company?'

The concept of compelling vision was developed for top managers but is equally useful lower down organizations. Managers need to understand the precise mission of their own departments, which may be different, although complementary, from the organization as a whole. The compelling vision concept is valid at the individual level, especially for those who are shaping their careers and reviewing their lifestyles. Once people realize its value, the compelling vision concept is applicable to many aspects of personal and professional life.

In summary, the key steps to establishing a vision of the future are:

1 Identify what kind of organization you are at the moment.
   What is your existing strategic driving force?
   What do you set out to be?
   What do you put your resources into?

What are you good at?
What do you do badly?
Why do you exist?

2   Explore the options for the future.
What resources do you have?
What are your valuable competences?
What is your competition good at?
If present trends continue, what will happen?
Where are there opportunities?
What level of risk is associated with each option?
How radical is each option?

3   Choose a single strategic vision.
What criteria will you use to choose your strategic driving force?
What needs to be done to ensure that a vision will be fully tested?
How will it affect decision making?
How often should review take place?
What must you do better and stop doing?

Anyone about to create something must have a vision of what they are aiming to achieve. So a gardener looking at the rubble-strewn plot of his new house will evaluate different possible layouts, then refine an image of how he wants the finished garden to look. Thereafter, all his gardening is devoted to turning the vision into a reality. A large garden requires extra help, so an organization must be created. The enthusiast must then find ways to enable his helpers to share in the overall vision. Identical principles apply to creating and renewing organizations. Leaders must be able to visualize the end result, then find ways of engaging the energy and enthusiasm of many others. We will discuss some of the ways that this can be done in the next chapter.

Is lack of a compelling vision a blockage in your organization?

The following activities from the companion volume, *50 Activities for Unblocking Organizational Communication* are especially relevant:

4   Personal visioning.
5   Clarifying values.
6   Formulating a compelling vision.

Persuasive management

Being attractive: managers encouraging people to follow.

In the mid-1970s an international motor manufacturer was in desperate trouble. Its products were outdated and the company had a 'haemorrhage of losses'. There was no shortage of analysis of the corporate malaise. It was widely agreed that the enterprise was poorly managed, over-manned, riddled with industrial relations problems and lacking an attractive product range.

A new chief executive tackled these problems with technical precision and earthy practicality. Millions were spent on recruiting a high quality team to develop a new car. Most importantly, the chief executive was deeply concerned about the attitudes of work people who could sabotage any hope of corporate recovery. The reality of the situation had to be fully explained to all employees. His philosophy of communication was 'I never threaten but I play the game of "consequences". I want people to know what the effect of their actions will be.'

When the long-awaited new model was ready to be launched, it was decided that every employee would see it and listen to a well-prepared presentation on the importance of the new car to the future of the company. Everyone would be inundated with management's message through all possible media. The new vehicles had to be reliably produced to high standards.

The communication programme largely achieved its objectives, and the car was outstandingly successful. One executive told me: 'The most remarkable thing is that we never did this before. Previous models were launched with a puff of hot air but we never pulled out all the stops to communicate. No one thought that it was worth the effort.'

As discussed in the previous chapter, there was a vision of this motor manufacturer's future deeply rooted in the members of the new top team. They understood the decision-making implications and knew how to feed their vision. For clarity and communication the vision was expressed as a mission statement. So far, so good. The top team then asked: 'What about all those who work for the organization?' They must feel part of the vision. It must become compelling. Management must influence: they must persuade.

Persuasion plays a vital role in enabling organizations to operate successfully. It does not happen by accident. A leading British industrialist, Michael Edwardes, emphasizes this point: 'People need to feel part of an overall strategy and feel they have some responsibility and involvement in decisions which affect them. No amount of table-thumping in the boardroom will achieve optimum performance from senior executives, middle managers or the shop floor if they do not understand the reasoning and accept some responsibility.' (Michael Edwardes, *Back from the Brink*, Collins, London 1983).

A compelling vision is a product of the corporate élite. To infuse an organization the vision must be spread outwards, like ink on blotting paper. The vision must guide decision making at every level. A strong sense of collective identity is an essential requirement. The vision of the future is impotent until communicated. People must be attracted to give their commitment and energy.

To help us understand the importance of sharing a compelling vision, consider a story told by an American magazine publisher at a managerial conference.

> After college I published several weekly newspapers...as we grew the printer often failed to meet his deadline. Therefore, I decided to establish my own printing plant. I called a major press manufacturer and ordered a quarter of a million dollar press. Much to my surprise they took the order with a $2000 deposit. The press was to be delivered in 45 days and during that time I would have to raise

> approximately $100,000 for the press, working capital and other equipment.... I accomplished this goal with a simple formula. First, I believed it could be done. Second, I believed it could be done within the time period set. Third, I was consumed with accomplishing the task. Fourth, I told all with whom I came in contact of my goal and asked for their help. What happened was phenomenal! It seemed that everyone I told could recognise my enthusiasm...their minds would go to work immediately...with each new person I approached, my enthusiasm grew and he also became consumed with enthusiasm. A secret goal cannot benefit from the participation and the force of others. A well-defined goal, shared with others and sparked with enthusiasm, will draw energy and forces that cannot be measured or suppressed.

Communication of the organization's vision of the future seems to be most effective when expressed directly and personally. Raymond Lygo, as the new admiral in charge of the aircraft carrier *Ark Royal*, was asked if he wished to talk to the ship's crew over the closed circuit television system. He said: 'I wouldn't dream of it. I want to do it face to face and see their eyes. If you are sheltering behind TV they can give you a raspberry.'

Trying to communicate a strategic vision is fraught with problems. One organization spent many thousands of pounds indentifying a corporate mission. Top management puzzled in endless weekend seminars; corporate creeds were drafted and crawled over word by word. Then the chairman made a video film called 'The Meaning and Goals of our Company'. Everyone in the organization was subjected to a tidal wave of communication but almost all reacted with scepticism, closely followed by cynicism. Why? The message was perceived to be full of 'weasel' words which were opposite to real behaviour from the top managers. One employee commented: 'Words are cheap. We've heard it all before. It's all very well for the boss to give us all the crap about how things are going to change. I'll believe it when it actually makes a difference to me.'

In a way, managers bring such problems on themselves. They lack the skills to persuade people to devote themselves to organizational goals. One senior manager commented: 'By putting employees, especially managers, into watertight compartments we incur great costs long term. They don't understand the broad picture and so tend to look after their own narrow interests. Everyone must be persuaded that the competitive position is always pre-eminent and they must think about how they can sustain it. We must make constant reference back to what we are about.'

Persuasion is concerned with shaping, reinforcing and changing attitudes, but is only effective when people are induced to abandon one set of behaviours and adopt different ones. Persuasion, by definition, is not directly coercive; it is a process of influence.

From management's viewpoint, the main purpose of persuasion is to generate a willing climate which supports the compelling vision. Willingness is built over time. It gives permission for managers to manage. If willingness does not exist, like the political situation in some parts of Northern Ireland or South Africa, then the whole fabric breaks down. Once destroyed, it can take years, even generations, for willingness to be rebuilt.

For a message to persuade it has to compete with other media for attention. Communication is around us every minute of the day: a slogan flashed by a neon tube, an impeccably typed memorandum pinned on an office noticeboard or the wink of a long-lashed eye are all communications. They tell us something about the world around us. Inputs bombard us through every sense. To confuse the situation further our deeply hidden inner self is constantly sending messages to our consciousness. The receiver of communication is constantly evaluating data, assessing what is important and trying to read between the lines.

Everyone is subjected to a tremendous variety of expertly presented communication. Clear and stimulating newspaper articles, professionally slick television, brilliant use of colour and visual images, and skilled presenters are commonplace. But mere slickness is not enough. Those who wish to be persuasive cannot assume that their targets are mindless sheep who will be seduced by an attractive presentation. People are persuaded when they feel that ideas are expressed by someone with integrity. As we discuss further in the chapter on 'High Trust', to be persuasive managers must be trusted.

Effective persuasion is based on good understanding of the target group. For this reason it is vital to acquire effective ways to take the organization's temperature and keep an eye on the patient. Managers, unlike politicians or musicians, have few involuntary ways to get feedback on how they are perceived. Unless they undertake attitude surveys or intensively canvas opinions it is natural for managers to look to their peers for reaffirmation, thereby ignoring the thoughts and feelings of those below. This is obviously hazardous. The importance of maintaining an upward flow of communication is an important topic (see chapter on 'Upward Flow').

Attitudes

Managers often wish to form or change attitudes, and to persuade people to devote their energy to achieving particular results. This means that they must influence the emotional life of their followers. Successful persuasion requires competence and skills quite different from logical decision-making abilities.

Attitudes only exist within the human mind but are very powerful determinants of how people behave. They give us internal standards to assess situations. All of us have experienced the restaurant waiter who really wants his customers to enjoy the meal and his unpleasant colleague who is only interested in leering at pretty girls. Both waiters may have identical skills but their attitudes make all the difference.

Attitudes, once formed, are resistant to change for the following reasons:

1   Attitudes form in childhood so they become 'built in' to us. We feel that out identity would be threatened if we ceased to hold our cherished attitudes.
2   Attitudes become dependent on each other so that there is a complex intertwined network. It is difficult for someone to change one element without affecting all the other beliefs which are dependent on it.
3   Attitudes are reinforced and supported by the social group that surrounds us. We are encouraged to believe that which our family, friends and colleagues believe. It is difficult to go out of line.

4   With age our attitudes tend to become firmer and more resistant to change. There is some truth in the adage 'You can't teach an old dog new tricks'.

5   When attitudes are attacked people tend to react defensively and, paradoxically, attitudes can thereby be strengthened. So attempts to influence may be counterproductive.

Despite the difficulties, managers will do what they can to mould their employees' attitudes. This means that the resistances described above will need to be overcome whenever possible. Without comment on the ethical implications of psychological manipulation there are fifteen persuasion techniques available to those in leadership positions.

Fifteen persuasion techniques

1   When selecting personnel for important positions appoint only those whose attitudes are positive.

2   Use training as a deliberate technique for indoctrinating employees. Ensure that training staff have the skills to handle this aspect of the job. It is especially important to reach new staff before they have been exposed to the organization.

3   Remove, weaken or displace those who are influential in leading others against the existing management approach.

4   Consolidate attitude change in small group discussions which are expertly led. This is the most reliable way to facilitate attitude change. (Consider the success of the Weight Watchers organization.)

5   Ensure that people 'know the enemy' so that they feel that they have someone to fight against. This also reduces criticism of leaders.

6   Develop a leader who is a father figure in whom people feel trust and give their loyalty. (This does not have to be a male; during the 1983 British election campaign Margaret Thatcher was repeatedly described as 'the best man we've got'.)

7   Reward conformity so that people are motivated to accept the organization's beliefs and values.
8   People are, in various ways, open to suggestion and leaders can use this vulnerability as a tool. Senior managers link management beliefs with 'good things' and develop their image as wise and especially capable individuals.
9   Effective persuaders use changes in the social and political environment to support their messages. They link themselves with respected authorities. People thereby feel that they are being led progressively.
10   Avoid over-dramatic presentations, which are often discounted or ignored. Maintain a credible but interesting image.
11   Warn of the consequences of non-acceptance of the management's viewpoint. Avoid threatening as this may provoke aggressive defence.
12   Keep repeating your message so that it is heard time and time again. This increases the chance of successful attitude change.
13   Present views in a conducive atmosphere which will be enjoyable. Attractive environments increase receptivity.
14   Emphasize a simple and clear message. People often want the world to be straightforward and understandable. Try to instil the essence of your viewpoint and put it across clearly.
15   Contact people through all of their senses. Use visual aids, which can have great effect.

These are the guidelines for effective persuasion which have been practised by leaders and studied by psychologists. Sometimes such persuasive techniques have been used for destructive, unethical or valueless purposes. Like all tools, the capacity to persuade may be used for good or ill. However, management persuasion is especially important because there may be other forces within an organization attempting to win the hearts and minds of the workforce.

Persuasion through action

The techniques described above are potent tools, but they are not sufficient. People are persuaded by stories, myths and legends which become more real than reality itself. In fact, story-telling and myth-making are the keys to persuasive communication. Consider these stories:

Ren Zephiropoulos of Versatec on his first day as manager of a new facility bought two gallons of paint and painted out the name labels on the executive reserved parking places.

A personnel director took a booklet from his briefcase. It was rainbow-coloured and jazzy, with the title 'Employee Handbook'. The personnel director said: 'It doesn't look like a big deal, but it means a lot. Every previous publication to staff looked like it was designed by the Soviet Ministry of Supply in 1954. The design of the brochure and our decision to be open and unbureaucratic has shocked people. The brochure says that: "things have changed".' One of his listeners said: 'That proves to me, once again, the importance of symbolism in communication.'

Ray Kroc of McDonalds found a fly at large in a Winnipeg franchise. Two weeks later the franchisee lost his franchise.

The quality control director of Unical Laboratories, a pharmaceutical company, was woken at midnight by a phone call from the owner of a retail drug store. He was told that one bottle of tablets appeared to have absorbed moisture. By seven the next day he was knocking on the door of the drug store owner's house. The problem was quickly solved and later that day the owner remarked: 'Those people at Unical really care. The QC boss drove eighty miles to see me before dawn today. He could have asked me to put the faulty tablets in the post. But no. That guy really put himself out.'

The managing director of a company with a three billion dollar turnover personally took every complaint call from customers for a week.

Once a month the chief executive of a large brewery spends a full day on the road delivering beer. He lifts barrels, drives the truck, talks to customers and tries to work fast enough to get the productivity bonus.

Stories like these are especially persuasive because they deal with real causes and effects. No one can pass off such a story as mere media hype. Stories are encapsulations of reality and their symbolic meaning is profound.

Astute managers create opportunities for stories to be told about them. A new story is generated each time a top corporate executive vists a distant site and recalls the name of the security officer or holds open a door for an over-encumbered electrician. Such stories coalesce into myths which determine how management is really perceived.

Managers can generate myths about themselves which are paradoxical. They are perceived as strong but responsive, approachable but incisive, humane but clinical, scientific but intuitive, cautious but lucky, and so on. Myths are rooted in the real character of people, but magnify aspects of their personality. Myths are the way powerful figures are humanized.

Stories are much more powerfully persuasive than speeches or pronouncements and so managers must find ways to create stories which support their compelling vision. For example, the Wang company prides itself on closeness to the customer. In one of its international operations a new chief executive was walking around the loading bay and he heard a telephone ringing persistently. A loader was sitting by the phone eating a sandwich. The new executive asked: 'Aren't you going to answer the phone?' The reply, 'He can phone back after lunch', was taken silently. A week later the loader was gone and everyone who heard the story realized once again that Wang expected its employees to demonstrate that the customer comes first.

We can now return to the theme that opened this chapter. Persuasion is needed to give a vision its compelling quality. The compelling vision, once persuasively communicated, becomes the force which shapes the organization. Everyone then uses it to set priorities, objectives and allocate resources. Marketing specialists communicate the vision to customers, buyers use it to govern their relationship with suppliers and work people devote their energies to make the vision a reality. Unless the compelling vision is shared, the organization will drift whilst others, driven by a clearer vision, steal the competitive advantage.

Is unpersuasive management a blockage in your organization?

The following activities from the companion volume, *50 Activities for Unblocking Organizational Communication*, are particularly relevant:

7   Communicating the compelling vision.
8   Tiers of objectives.
9   Storytelling.
10   Rewards in furniland.
11   Influencing style audit.
12   How do we persuade?

Integrating the effort

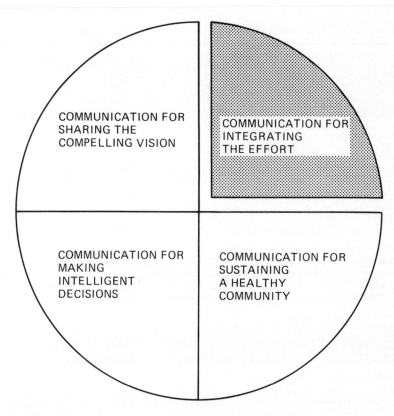

'Energy and effort pushing in the same direction.'

Definitions

Integration – 'to combine parts or elements into a whole'
Effort – 'a strenuous exertion of power, physical or mental'

Shorter Oxford Dictionary

Integrating mechanisms

Being co-ordinated: adequate mechanisms to integrate effort.

Some years ago there was a major accident at sea. A tanker was swept onto the rocks and vast quantities of oil began to spurt from her ruptured tanks. Huge quantities of anti-pollution chemicals were urgently required. In just a few days, supplies were manufactured and moved to the decontamination fleet. Small manufacturers reacted quickly. Whilst large companies mulled over their production capacities, tender prices and delivery arrangements, it was chemical companies with a few dozen workers who delivered a quotation and co-ordinated manufacture within hours.

Organizations elaborate their structures as they grow. Adam Smith, one of the first observers of the effects of industrialization on patterns of work, made his classic study of a group of pin-makers. He explained that, using division of labour, the group's output was vastly greater than a similar number of isolated people completing all of the tasks themselves. Division of labour is the key to the efficiency of the factory system, but creates a need to ensure that people work together to achieve the desired overall results. A large proportion of organizational communication is concerned with achieving integration.

Consider a straightforward example. College lecturers are all specialists: one in industrial law, another in taxation accounting, a third in management policy and so on. Students require an integrated course, and so college lecturers must co-ordinate their work together. Mechanisms for doing this include timetables, syllabuses, meetings, policy statements, informal contact and managerial responsibility. Much of the day-by-day communication between college lecturers is concerned with maintaining integration. In more complex environments, like the armed services at war, a phenomenal amount of communication is needed to orchestrate many different resources. In fact, the need for integration varies according to the size of the organization and the tasks undertaken.

The size of the organization is the first variable. There are clear distinctions between pioneer enterprises and large organizations. A small concern, normally directed and energized by a leader with a compelling vision has relatively few problems of integration. Everyone can be gathered in one room! Employees are carefully selected; co-ordination is relatively simple. Shared understanding leads to communication being open and efficient. However, growth brings disintegration and crisis. Primitive systems fail to cope with increasing complexity. The remedy is to introduce scientific management; systems, procedures, rational organization and experts which provide a comprehensible framework for integration. With this in place, further organizational growth can proceed.

Despite elaborate and specialized systems, scientific management does not result in a 'bed of roses'. Logic, structures, procedures and expertise contain the seeds of a new malaise. Gradually, overhead costs rise, red tape proliferates, and vital spontaneity is lost. Communication becomes convoluted and turgid as procedures replace initiative and defensive walls are built between specialist departments. The organization suffers the same fate as an overgrown garden choked with weeds. Massive attempts must be made to eliminate the effects of creeping bureaucracy.

The degree of precision and complexity required by the task is the second variable. A jazz band relies on the players being alert to each other and constantly adjusting their music in the general direction of the tune. A similarly sized musical group, a string quartet, has a more precise task and depends on careful adherence to a musical score (which is the primary integrating mechanism) to perform a Mozart piece. A large organization with a precise and complex task, like a symphony orchestra, requires more managerial integration and so invariably defers to the direction of a conductor.

Large organizations are essential to perform complex tasks (like mass-producing motor cars) or benefiting from economies of scale (like oil refining). They have five distinct specialisations:

1 Operators   who do the work.
2 Managers   who direct, control and co-ordinate.
3 Analysts   who innovate, standardize and rationalize processes.
4 Support staff who enable work to proceed.
5 Directors   who establish the direction of the organization, make key decisions and monitor performance.

Complex systems are developed by analysts and implemented by middle managers. Top management have the task of making key decisions, allocating resources and evaluating performance. Operators have the simple task of performing their specified roles. Managers struggle with many complexities as they turn objectives into action programmes.

Often total simplification is impossible and communication systems become extremely elaborate. Consider a production department making small batches of complex equipment which require hundreds of parts, each ordered from specialist suppliers with varying lead times. Tens of thousands of interdependent movements take place in a typical week. Meanwhile, in the development department, bright engineers are changing designs, then changing the changes. Production workers swap parts to meet urgent needs and confuse the record keepers. All this adds to the complexity. Economic considerations compel cost-conscious managers to seek reductions in expensive stocks and keep investment to a minimum. Over-ordering, the easy way of dealing with such problems, is unacceptable. Managers faced with such problems develop techniques for controlling the situation, even developing a special language with precise concepts like 'tentative stock orders', 'stock simulation reports', 'sequencing protocols', and 'change concessions'. Such concepts are essential mechanisms for integration even though they may appear an esoteric mystique of specialists.

Organizations devote substantial resources to coping with such problems. As more 'senders' are included within a communication network, so the complexity increases. For example, if only two individuals communicate they require just one communication channel. Five different senders require ten channels. If we increase this to 100 (not an unusual situation in organizations) then the number of channels required becomes 4,950. A thousand senders of information will require 495,000 channels of communication to ensure that each can talk to the others. The mushrooming complexity of communication in large organizations can only be dealt with by systems and specialization. Computer control of complex systems permits a level of integration previously impossible. Man could not journey to the moon until computers became available. Unfortunately the interdependence of elements increases the need for the whole system to work at levels of effectiveness previously unachieved. Massive breakdowns with horrendous complications become more possible. The risks of failure are catastrophic, so considerable investment in sustaining effective integration despite equipment malfunction is essential.

Disintegration is sometimes critical. The most dramatic examples are military. Consider an experience which taught Napoleon an important lesson. In the first portion of the Waterloo campaign Napoleon's army was divided into two parts. The right wing, commanded by the Emperor himself, faced Blucher at Ligny; the left wing, under Marshal Ney, faced Wellington at Quatre Bras. Both Ney and the Emperor prepared to attack, planning the use of a third force, led by Erlon, to help deliver a final blow. Because Napoleon and Marshall Ney failed to communicate their plans, and because orders were unclear, Erlon spent the day marching back and forth between the two fields without engaging in the action of either.

Organizational types

An effective organization is both specialized and integrated. How can managers tackle the crucial task of choosing the best organization? It is now widely understood that the question,

'What is the best way to organize?' has only one valid answer: 'It depends on what you want to organize to do.' Knowledge about the best ways to organize enables managers to make judgements on the basis of expertise, as a surgeon, rather than hunches and experience, like a magician.

Management structures are selective in the communication they transmit. Functional structures develop excellence in technical specialisms but tend to be poor in integrating the work of different functions. Product-based structures often have the opposite weakness: they fail to sustain real specialist capability. Specific patterns of communication are needed to tackle particular tasks. To understand how communication is related to organization we need some way of defining particular organizational types. This is an important but somewhat complex topic and I acknowledge that much of the following discussion is based on the brilliant work of Professors Mintzberg and Galbraith. (See H. Mintzberg, *Structuring in Fives*, Prentice-Hall, Englewood Cliffs, New Jersey, 1983; and J. R. Galbraith, *Designing Complex Organizations*, Addison-Wesley, Reading, Mass. 1973.)

Following Henry Mintzberg's analysis, there are five distinct types of organizations. We will consider each, briefly describe its characteristics, and consider the implications for organizational communication.

1 Simple structure

This is a small (or crisis-ridden) organization, often in its pioneer stage, ruled by one or two people. It is controlled by direct supervision of the boss. Often a family firm, the simple structure is flexible, unformalized and autocratic. Many small businesses (or organizations in crisis) thrive under clear 'hands-on' leadership by a boss. Complexity, excess staff, over-elaborate systems and formality are enemies. The boss takes decisions, seizes opportunities and aggressively confronts the world. But beware! The simple structure is the most risky of all, as it depends on the health and drive of one person. Also, expansion is limited, since the lack of formal organization prevents large tasks from being managed.

Effective communication in the simple structure requires that the boss knows every key employee. Information is conveyed to the boss, who is the hub of the wheel – in the centre of everything. It is imperative that the centralized decision taker knows precisely what is going on. Flexibility and decisiveness are key, as is a sense of mission. The boss is the only person who can convey direction and objectives to the workforce.

2 Machine bureaucracy

This is an organization based on rules, procedures, systems and controls. It is controlled by precise specification of work processes. As far as possible, people are used as interchangeable elements in complex systems, trained to behave like cogs in a well-oiled wheel. Organizations, like airlines or post offices, have many routine tasks to perform predictably time and time again. Tasks become highly specialized. Rules and regulations abound. Communication is formalized and elaborate. Different functions have their own managers who are expert in their discipline. Specialists, like work study analysts, accountants, quality controllers and planners proliferate. Without them the organization would collapse into inefficient chaos. Managers are 'obsessed with control', seeking to measure all variables and eliminate uncertainties.

Although the machine bureaucracy is technically efficient, there are latent conflicts which threaten productivity. Controls and disciplines are dehumanizing and tensions mount. Often management can only ameliorate or bottle up potential trouble.

Communication is essential for control. Managers must develop sophisticated systems to collect data, monitor performance and set up systems of rules and procedures. Communication serves to increase conformity. Discipline is all important. The manager in a machine bureaucracy must communicate formal systems and disciplines in ways which ordinary people will accept. Transgressions need to be dealt with effectively. Enlightened managements in such organizations do what they can to help people find meaning in their work (see chapter on 'Supportive Teamwork'). Although the character of the organization diminishes motivation, effective communication can mitigate some of the harmful effects of treating people like machines.

3   Professional bureaucracy

This is an organization where the most important work is carried out by professionals. It is controlled by selecting and training competent individuals. A hospital is a good example. The organization supports the work of professional doctors and surgeons. Police forces, universities, hospitals and accounting firms all require highly-skilled individuals able to meet complex but predictable requirements. There is much delegation of decision making.

This type of organization is dependent on the competence of skilled workers who must be trusted to do the job in a professional way. All doctors can be expected, hopefully, to go through a thorough diagnosis when a patient arrives with a complaint, but the subsequent treatment varies from patient to patient. Doctors cannot be supervised or programmed all the time – that would be vastly expensive and counter-productive – so the organization provides an environment which sets basic standards and then enables highly-trained professionals to get on with their work. In professional bureaucracies there is an enormous amount of training and education. Professional skills and attitudes take years to accumulate and must be regularly updated.

Those in management roles have to avoid simplistic rule-making or its opposite, abdication. They need to develop a steering and co-ordinating role. Power is largely decentralized and managerial leadership is persuasive rather than autocratic. For this reason it is difficult to determine corporate strategy.

Although professional bureaucracies provide deeply satisfying work for individuals, the lack of a strong central organization means that decision making emerges from political intrigue. Influence rather than reason may rule the day. Also, independent professionals sometimes abuse their position by laziness or unethical conduct. Innovation, which requires the co-operation of colleagues, is notoriously difficult to orchestrate. In fact, creative thinking often fails to flourish as such organizations work along time-proven lines. The difficulty of obtaining the willing co-operation of many independent people means that change proceeds with almost painful slowness. It is difficult to manage by objectives since outputs are intangible. However, despite all of the disadvantages, organizations which ask people to perform varied and complex tasks have no option but to place control in the hands of the operator. Nothing else has been proven to work.

Much communication in the professional bureaucracy is affected by the personalities of senders and receivers. Relationships between professional and support services can be tense. Senior management must communicate clearly with full explanations of reasons. A professional consensus is essential if top managers' decisions are to be supported.

4 Divisionalized form

This is a large organization which has divided operations into manageable units. Each division is controlled by careful measurement of outputs. Divisions become the operating units, each serving a distinct market. As each division is largely independent, much authority and responsibility are delegated to divisional management teams. Most large profit-making organizations since the Second World War have evolved specialized divisions to suit particular markets. The divisionalized form pushes decision making downwards and duplicates functions – every division has a full complement of analysts and experts. It is expensive in overheads but allows units to be profit centres and independently measurable. Headquarters allow much freedom but carefully monitor results. Much day-by-day authority is given to unit managers whose skills are critical, so training and indoctrination are vital to ensure consistently high-quality decision making.

Communication is focused on results. Divisions develop their own goals and negotiate with headquarters. Quantitative measures are required; without them control cannot be exercised. A sympathetic use of both carrot and stick best describes the relationship between headquarters and division. Headquarters maintain control over strategic planning, allocate financial resources, establish control systems, appoint key personnel, conduct basic research and form broad policies. The divisions focus attention on markets they know and are able to be decisive.

The divisionalized form is one solution to a problem of red tape. Huge monolithic bureaucracies, structured like spiders' webs, are ponderous, stultifying and maladaptive. The divisionalized form of organization enables people to thrive and take initiatives to succeed (or not) on the basis of their own efforts.

The divisionalized form of structure has its costs. Sometimes units devote scarce resources repeating work which another part of the organization has already undertaken; or large projects requiring economies of scale are not undertaken because people 'think small'. Communication in the divisionalized form has the following negative characteristics:

○ divisional management tends to develop protective mechanisms against headquarters
○ divisions tend to become exclusive and not share objectives with sister units
○ overall strategy is difficult to convey as divisions are concerned with the threats and opportunities of the moment
○ much communication with headquarters is formalized, dealing with financial information, which means that top management can be out of touch.

5 Adhocracy

This is an organization which operates in a complex and turbulent world where innovation is essential. It is controlled by discussion between experts. Rigid organizations are incapable of giving the flexibility needed for a high level of creativity. Accordingly, an organization is needed which is organic and changes shape according to current needs. The solution is an adhocracy. Bureaucracy is consciously avoided. Teams tackle particular projects and then disband. Individuals are encouraged to follow their own interests. An incredible amount of co-ordination is necessary to derive something productive from the mêlée of creative activity.

If the task is to build a new generation computer, manufacture prototypes or manage a rock group then throw away the formal options and devise an adhocracy. This requires breaking away from established patterns, and not relying on standardization or formalization which would stifle creativity. Adhocracies need to be open with frequent meetings and frequent reviews. Clear job demarcations, invariable routines and rigid disciplines are unhelpful. All manner of communication techniques are vital to co-ordinate work. Change is often needed: in the first eight years of its life, the American NASA organization changed its structure seventeen times. As bureaucracy increased in NASA it became vulnerable to defective decision making (see chapter on 'Upward Flow').

Adhocracies grow complex and untidy – often using the two boss matrix concept – yet such structural untidiness is essential to their innovative power. Managers develop skills in handling bewildering and divergent situations. They become expert co-ordinators and resource allocators. Power is held by those who have expertise rather than formal bosses. Top management has the role of accumulating resources and reassigning specialists to the needs of the moment. Strategy is reviewed many times as new facts emerge. Action planning from the top may actually impede achievement since only the originators of projects know enough to get them done. Top managers spend much time identifying strategic options and deciding between highly complex arguments. They try to control, but can often only intervene after the event when the money has already been spent.

Some of the most innovative firms are adhocracies. Two examples are Bell Laboratories in the United States and Sinclair Research Limited in England, both of which designed world-beating products. Such organizations tend to be most dramatically creative in their youth but, as we all know, youth is a time of high energy but suspect decision making.

Communication in an adhocracy is all important. Much informal contact must be maintained, and any conflict brought out into the open to find the best answers to tough questions. Liaison channels and temporary teams are crucial. In fact, there is a danger of overwhelming the system with communication.

Integrating mechanisms

We have just defined five types of organization, all of which can be viable. Many people are deeply cynical about organizations, regarding them as inevitable but essentially undesirable. Yet this popular view is deeply unfair. Organizations are the most powerful tool known to man. We have no other means of combining the human talents and resources to get complex things done. An effective organization is a supreme example of man's achievement – as valuable as a work of art or a world record in athletics.

The design of an organization is determined as managers ask these questions:

> What are we aiming to achieve?
> What must we do to get there?
> How do we control what is going on?
> How do we exploit the talents of people?
> What must we be really good at doing?
> How can we evaluate our progress?

The answers to these questions enable an organizational structure to be determined which establishes the major specialisms and where power is located. Between the specialisms there must be integrating mechanisms.

Exactly which mechanisms for integration are needed only comes from a careful analysis of the tasks being undertaken. Consider a typical new product. The specification is determined by the marketing department, who invite the research function to contribute new ideas and then development engineers devise a prototype. Once proven, this passes to a pre-production department which prepares it for the manufacturing department. The product begins to be made and then passes into the hands of test engineers before going into store. Meanwhile the packaging department, training department, advertising department, quality department and the health and safety officers have all made their contribution. Finally the product goes into the salesman's hands before, hopefully, being purchased by a customer. But it does not end there. A service department and market research department continue to be concerned with the subsequent use of the product. In a large organization perhaps twenty separate departments are involved in the manufacture of a single product. They have to work together efficiently and speedily; their efforts must be integrated.

Integration is difficult because each department has distinct aims. Research scientists are interested in the far reaches of technology, production managers want predictability and salesmen seek products which are demonstrably better than their competitors'. Some departments' aims are almost incompatible with others. Communication is bound to be fractious.

There are two approaches to developing greater integration. First, management can improve existing mechanisms or create new ones. Secondly, those within the organization, from top to bottom, can be helped to analyse their needs and find practical ways of resolving them. Both approaches have disadvantages. The first suffers through possible over-simplification, while the second 'grass roots' philosophy can lack coherence and logic.

Whichever approach is used, the end result will be the same. 'Integrating mechanisms' will manage the interfaces between key individuals and departments. The more complex the integration requirement, the more emphasis needs to be placed on effective mechanisms. Galbraith's list of ten integrating mechanisms begins with the simplest at the top (see J. R. Galbraith, *Designing Complex Organizations*, Addison-Wesley, Reading, Mass. 1973).

1 Direct supervision – one person is given the task of co-ordinating several different people's work.
2 Standardization of people – ensures that only trained people are allowed to do the job.
3 Standardization of processes – lays down procedures to determine what should be done.
4 Standardization of outputs – sets clear objectives and success measures.
5 Direct contact – managers get together to resolve problems informally.
6 Liaison roles – someone is appointed to act as liaison officer.
7 Task teams – multi-disciplining teams are established to co-ordinate a specific activity.
8 Integrating manager – authority given to a manager who has the power to ensure that liaison takes place.
9 Product organization – separate organizations established to manufacture a single product or service.

10   Matrix organization – both product and specialisation are managed.

Each of the ten integrating mechanisms described above demands management action and Professor Galbraith has brilliantly spelt out the possibilities. For an illustration from my own experience, consider the seventh mechanism, task teams. One morning a group assembled in a conference room to form an action group and manage the transformation of an unused railway siding into a technology park. There were representatives from industry, local government, banks, and architects. It was fascinating to see how they established the basis for integrating their efforts. These were the questions asked:

1   Identify a leader
    Who will be the leader?
    What is the leader's role?
    What kind of powers will the leader have (does he 'have teeth')?
2   Identify the members of the action group
    What are the names of active group members?
    What contribution will each make to the project?
    How can they be contacted?
    Are there any limitations on their involvement?
    Who will pay for expenses?
3   Specify pattern of meetings
    Who will meet?
    Who will call meetings?
    How often will meetings be held?
    What is the status of meetings?
    What happens if a member of the action group cannot attend?
4   Clarify information system
    Who supplies information to whom?
    How often is this done?
    In what form should the information be given?
    What data-handling facilities are needed?
    How open and honest are people expected to be?
5   Establish a communication 'node'
    Who co-ordinates the information?

> Who can answer questions?
> How will records be kept?
> Who has access to the records?
> Who makes and circulates notes of meetings?

The action group went through all of these key questions. They looked at the overall task and developed procedures for integrating their contributions. Information channels had to be specified. All available tools – meetings, reports, telephone, telex, fax, management information systems etc. – were used.

Sometimes the task team (mechanism 7) is too weak. Then the eighth mechanism, an integrating manager, may be appropriate. Consider this example: an electronics company won a huge contract to supply low cost battlefield radars to a foreign government. The chief executive realized that there were opportunities to sell the equipment to other countries, but it would be necessary to repackage the radars as commercial products. The company was functionally organized so the commercial adaptation of the battlefield radar, codenamed 'Crow', proceeded in a piecemeal fashion. No one was put in overall charge but much money was expended in engineering and marketing. The chief executive became increasingly concerned as deadlines were not met. He held a meeting and heard many comments like these:

> 'We are poor at creating new products.'
> 'We have fallen into the trap of overspecifying the product and under-planning.'
> 'No one seems to own the problems.'
> 'There are a lot of brick walls.'
> 'Some departments show glee when others get in the brown stuff.'
> 'If we were able to communicate, then we would have a business that can take off.'

The chief executive, belatedly, realized that there were serious problems in the power structure of the company. Someone had to be responsible and accountable for the Crow project. This was a difficult decision, as appointing a product champion meant that functional managers would lose some of their power.

Also, the chief executive had to encourage co-operation and openness; the structure could be changed but it would not solve the problem unless people were willing to make the new structure work.

The Crow product champion was a well liked young engineer, Hilary Smith. She said afterwards: 'No one consciously wanted the Crow project to fail, but they had to be shown how to help. I planned the whole thing. Eventually, people felt that we were onto a winner and they joined.'

Hilary used the following devices for integration:

○ controlled the budget
○ made friends with important managers
○ set up lots of meetings
○ gave regular information on project progress
○ negotiated for resources
○ developed a sophisticated plan
○ acquired the information to enable control to be exercised
○ kept up-to-date with all changes.

Effective integrating mechanisms are vital. Six days a week the representatives of American and Russian forces meet in a small hut which sits on the border between North and South Korea. At exactly noon the representatives sit in their places across the table, but in different countries. At one time both sides played one-upmanship, carrying in bigger and bigger national flags that overfilled the hut. Then there was a meeting about flags and all returned to normal. A reporter, witnessing the regular meeting, had to stand with his arm in one country and his microphone in the other. Although the scene appears ludicrous, that table and the formality are an integrating mechanism and prevent incidents escalating into battles.

I began by referring to Adam Smith who first described the benefits of the division of labour. His work spelt out the vital importance of communication between specialists. This chapter has investigated the need for integration in organizations and administrative systems. The next chapter considers a further aspect of integration: physical layout.

Is a lack of integrating mechanisms a blockage in your organization?

The following activities from the companion volume, *50 Activities for Unblocking Organizational Communication*, are especially relevant:

13   Organizational types audit.
14   War room.
15   A nice day out.
16   Integrating mechanisms.

Helpful geography

Being convenient: the layout of the organization encourages necessary communication.

The executive board of Protronic, a rapidly expanding electronics company, had a tremendous reputation for innovative opto-electronics instruments. Senior executives were technical wizards who had striven for excellence. The world beat a path to their door. One morning they met to consider how to enlarge their production facility. Their existing site, an old shoe-polish factory, was overcrowded and highly-paid engineers went home complaining that they smelt like boot repairers. Senior managers occupied offices in the middle of the factory, and could see what was happening in the production areas. The executive board decided that the existing building did nothing for the image of the firm and they would spend their windfall profits by building superb new accommodation.

A fashionable architect proposed a new building site in a technology park. There would be a suite of executive offices in Hollywood style around a swimming pool and the production facility would be about 100 metres away, with the layout consciously designed for the best possible quality of working life. It was to be a model twenty-first-century work environment.

As the executive board started to debate the architect's layout plans, they received a large order to develop a military observation system called 'Watchdog'. The decision to move to the technology park was taken on the same evening that the

Watchdog order was confirmed. Construction proceeded quickly and Protronic moved to the new facilities. The executive teams were photographed proudly receiving an award for imaginative design. Two years later every member of the board agreed that the morning of the move was the first day of a prolonged disaster.

For several months all seemed to be going well. Executives worked all hours to complete the designs for Watchdog. They enjoyed the pool, having the occasional business meeting on a large floating mattress. Secretaries swam in the lunch hours and Vivaldi played softly through the office hi-fi system. Nothing was allowed to disturb the creative atmosphere. The initial designs were finished on schedule and the production department took over responsibility for manufacture. The executive team had a party and started work on the second phase of the project.

Meanwhile, across in the production building, serious problems began to occur, but it took months before senior management realized they had a crisis. The design proved virtually impossible to manufacture. Despite much emergency effort Watchdog was delivered fourteen months late and the penalty clauses nearly bankrupted the business. In a post-mortem meeting the chief executive said: 'We committed the worst sin in the book. We failed to keep in touch with the total job. That 100-metre divide between us and production was the big, big error. We carried on, in our own sweet way, whilst the place fell apart. As an act of penance I want us to leave the executive building, turn it into a leisure centre for staff, and get back into the heart of the business where we belong. This must never happen again.'

Local geography has a major influence on human communication. In the case described above, it became apparent that the isolation of executives, cocooned in their own building and floating on the swimming pool caused a communication blockage. Important information, which was previously absorbed through informal conversation, was lost. Unhelpful geography led to organizational disintegration. As one engineer put it: 'After the move, it was like a man whose brain ceases to know what his body is doing. He was badly burnt without realizing it.'

The word 'geography' is defined as 'the physical environment within which the organization operates. Environment includes buildings, layout, materials used, noise, privacy, communal areas, symbolic messages from buildings, juxtaposition of people and functions and the use of space.' In this chapter we will explore the effects of organizational geography on communication and consider what can be done to create 'helpful geography'.

Effects of geography

The effect of the physical environment on communication becomes obvious when you listen to a young executive describe how he prepares for a first date with a new girlfriend. He makes a special music tape for the car stereo which becomes increasingly smoochy as time goes by. He books the most discreet table at a romantic restaurant, and takes a rug so that they can sit comfortably on a dark hilltop looking for meteors. The young man understands, quite correctly, that the subtleties of the local environment make a real difference to the quality of human interaction.

People are greatly influenced by the physical environment in which they work. Train drivers sit isolated in their cabs, operators wear hearing protectors to avoid being deafened by the pounding of their machines, and managers congregate in congenial bars as the relaxed atmosphere helps them form into a team.

Those who design workplaces often appear to be unconscious of the psychological effects of their decisions. My friend Don Young told me about a proposal to change the layout in a fishfinger factory. 'The production engineers wanted to establish isolated work stations, where women would work packing fish into boxes and there would be no possibility for conversation. This would have destroyed the community and taken the life out of the factory. In fact, the opposite was needed. The packers liked to chat as this overcame the monotony of the job. What looked efficient on the planner's drawings failed to consider the human element.'

Design has subtle effects. For example, buildings create a particular emotional atmosphere. Most people report that when they enter a cathedral they feel a sense of awe and reverence, even though they may be atheists. Visit the library of Harvard University and you feel respect for learning. A good pub has laughter embedded in the walls. Buildings either facilitate or inhibit work through their structures, layout, proportions, décor, lighting and history.

The psychological effects of environment can be unexpected. For example, there is strong evidence that colour affects emotions and moods. Psychologists have observed that some depressed people are helped by staring at a yellow card for a few minutes. Hospital operating theatres are predominantly green, as this has proved to be an easy colour to live with. On the negative side, the dirty grey of weathered concrete gives an impression of soulless decay.

Environment evokes feelings and emotion, and can become a barrier to communication. I recall the first occasion I had a meeting at the Palace of Westminster. The grandeur and sense of occasion were confidence-sapping. Later, with familiarity, the same physical environment became comfortable and uninhibiting. Symbolic messages sent by buildings are well understood by some retailers who brilliantly construct their stores to be exciting and inviting. Colours, sounds, layout, shape and image all go together to give a statement of what the shop is all about. Such messages are the physical manifestations of the compelling vision of the organization.

Some managers are very aware of the 'message' that a building sends to its employees and the outside world. One of Britain's largest companies, Imperial Chemical Industries, occupied large, monolithic headquarters near the Houses of Parliament. On a television programme, the chairman, John Harvey Jones, explained his argument for moving like this: 'This is a beautiful office' – he waves a hand at the walnut panelling – 'but it gives out the wrong messages. We are supposed to be a lean and hungry company. This creates the impression of a company which is mighty, powerful and unchanging; in other words a British institution. Any company that thinks it is a British institution is on the way out.'

The fact that buildings give a message to the world has been realized by some government agencies who abandoned their huge, impersonal office blocks and set up small and informal neighbourhood offices. The public is more likely to use bureaucratic services when they are both physically and psychologically accessible.

In order to understand the relationship between communication and the physical environment, it is important to consider how local geography is constructed. Buildings are designed by architects who are inclined to be idealistic and Utopian. In the main, they have been educated to think of their profession as an art form rather than a human service. The subtleties of human interaction have often been sacrificed in pursuit of an aesthetic ideal. Examples include receptionists isolated in greenhouse lobbies, managers eating in a leather-lined dining room and working in high prestige offices which encourage a false notion of their own omniscience; professional workers, whose work is intellectually demanding, are expected to be creative in noisy cubicles in open plan offices. It is ironic that some of the best environments for people were constructed before the profession of architecture was invented.

Much modern architecture is influenced by the work of a visionary, Le Corbusier, who preached functionalism and a complete break with tradition. Le Corbusier wanted to sweep away organic and diverse urban environments and build 'machines to live and work in'. His influence turned many architectural students into zealots who sought to change the human condition through redesigning the environment. Fortunately, such idealism is now on the wane as we have learnt that people need buildings which respect human nature and facilitate organic communication. However, Le Corbusier's ideas are still a powerful influence on those who design environments.

The enormous effects of local planners on human communication can be seen in inner-city areas where the old small houses have been bulldozed and replaced by huge concrete housing developments. In the old homes people lacked basic facilities but they had close feelings of identity with their neighbours. Huge developments have isolated people and weakened their sense of community. The consequences are increased vandalism, mental illness, crime, and profound dissatisfaction. One resident said it all: 'Having a matchbox in the sky cuts you off from others. People protect themselves from the outside world rather than be part of it.'

The lack of concern by architects for the effects of their work on organizational communication was shown in an interesting way. While researching for this chapter I approached several librarians at specialized architectural colleges in London and asked: 'What information do you have on the relationship between architecture and communication in organizations?' The librarians tried to be helpful, but there was little of value in their libraries. Countless shelves were full of books on functionalism, aesthetics, materials, drainage etc., but almost nothing on the intimate details of the 'man/building' interface.

How to improve geography

However, despite this jaundiced view of architects and urban planners, there are some studies which help us progress. The work of Jane Jacobs (*The Death and Life of Great American Cities*, Random House, New York, 1961) suggests how to create environments which encourage open communication. She says that five elements need to be present:

> Environments should be 'close textured' with a lot of different things going on.
> There should be high density occupation so that there are plenty of people around.
> People should meet often and informally, and slowly get to know each other.
> Distances should be relatively small so that communication is straightforward.
> People need their own space which is defensible. They need to feel ownership of an area.

This is an interesting list. It says that physical environments should be organic, and diverse and compact to meet deep human needs. Of course, Jane Jacobs was writing about cities, not productive organizations. We need to add another dimension – people should be helped by the local environment to integrate their work.

This analysis may seem abstract but has practical value. Consider the following example. In Britain during the opening months of the Second World War the RAF faced an almost impossible task. A huge force of German bombers and fighters were dedicated to 'bring Britain to its knees'. The RAF had few fighter planes and it would be many months before a strong defensive force could be built. It was imperative that the scant forces at their disposal were used to maximum effect. The survival of the nation was at stake.

Communication and co-ordination were all important. An air defence control room was established to provide all available information and decision-making resources in one place. The room was located to be both accessible and secure. A large map of England and Europe formed the centrepiece. On a raised platform sat the controllers who could see everything and were in direct communication with the war cabinet. The back wall was covered with display boards which showed the state of readiness of each fighter air station and weather conditions. WRAF staff stood around the map with telephone headsets to relay the positions of both enemy and defence planes. They moved symbols across the map to illustrate the attack patterns. This crucial information display was the end result of hundreds of observations by men and women who scanned the night sky from remote fields or watched the primitive radar displays. Each observer saw a small scrap of the whole but as the data was combined in the system it became possible to understand the overall situation.

As an attack developed the controllers saw the threat and ordered their fighter squadrons to respond. Accurate information was needed very quickly and it had to be displayed in the simplest possible way. Those in charge had to see all of the significant factors in one glance. Organizational geography has been designed to help them.

Other groups who are allowed to design their own environment find that the war room or command headquarters concept is the best way to manage control, communication and co-ordination on a minute-by-minute basis. From television we are all familiar with the NASA Space Mission Control Centre at Houston but, perhaps, we are less conscious that those television pictures are managed by a control room in the outside broadcast television unit that operates according to the same principles as mission control.

The war room is a technique for creating helpful geography.

However, despite our best endeavours, it is impossible to keep organizations organic. In recent years, to some extent, we have become capable of designing 'electronic helpful geography'. Modern technology has reduced some potential geographical barriers. The salesman, once isolated in his car, is now on a cellular telephone. Enthusiasts all around the world communicate through computerized bulletin boards. It is possible for executives in New York, Hamburg, Tokyo and London to talk face-to-face through a video conference link. Such technologies reduce or eliminate geographical barriers and permit organizations to be integrated despite becoming more dispersed.

The liberating effects of electronic communication are most vividly seen in the financial world. Stock exchanges used to be imposing buildings in which dealers conducted their business face-to-face. Now a stock exchange is fed by a network of interacting computers which span the world. In this case, barriers of geography and complexity have been largely overcome by the talents of systems designers. The financial world shows us what can be done where numerical data has to be transferred. Less readily quantifiable matters, like problem solving, planning and co-ordination, have proved to be less easily systemized. Here, for the time being, the human element remains dominant.

Devising helpful geographical environments can be considered on three levels. First, workplace design; secondly, team interaction, and lastly, at the whole organization level.

Workplace design

The design of a work area determines communication patterns. It was Bert Medlam, the production manager at the UK General Foods Plant, who taught me this lesson. Bert had worked on the shop floor and understood what it felt like to operate machinery month after month. New equipment was to be installed and Bert said: 'I don't want people being forced to live like hermits. All the control panels must be laid out so that the operators work together as a team.'

Bert was right. The operators worked better and had an improved quality of life when they were physically close. In fact, there are five disadvantages of unhelpful workplace design:

○ people are deprived of the necessary information to make job decisions
○ friendship and support of others is prevented
○ co-ordination with colleagues is undermined
○ the opportunity to learn new methods, concepts and skills is reduced
○ there are increased barriers to asking questions and expressing points of view.

The immediate environment can create barriers to communication in one or more of these five areas. Sometimes people can reduce such barriers if they take assertive steps for themselves. However, we live with the most inconvenient situations simply because we become used to them. A mundane example clarifies the point. Management meetings are often held in overheated rooms, so everyone feels drowsy and attention deteriorates. Yet it is rare for a window to be opened or a brisk walk taken. The inadequate environment is tolerated, even when someone actually falls asleep.

The following questions help raise people's consciousness of the effect that their immediate environment has on their communication with others:

How does *location* of your workplace influence your communication with others?

How does *noise* influence your communication with others?

How does your job environment provide adequate *informal meeting places*?

Does your job environment provide accessible *formal meeting places*?

Do you have adequate *access* to your manager and those you work with?

Does the normal *working atmosphere* encourage or discourage the kind of work that you do?

Are you able to *give opinions and ask questions* easily?

Communication requirements vary between individuals and jobs. The needs of an airline pilot are different to those of a commercial designer. We must examine each job and ask:

'What are the communication needs of any person performing this function?' Local geography should then be designed to help the job holder.

Team interaction

Integration requires contact between people whose work is interdependent. Imagine giving a few pieces of a jigsaw to fifty people at random located in different boroughs of a major city and asking them to complete the puzzle whilst going about their normal daily tasks. There is no doubt – the jigsaw will remain in pieces. Easy contact between people with interdependent work is essential for co-ordination.

All organizations have specialized departments, structured as teams. Work groups become as territorial as song birds, investing a great deal of effort in protecting their boundaries against encroachment from outsiders. Perhaps this is natural as our ancestors learned in the Stone Age that the 'hunting band' is the best way to ward off sabre-toothed tigers. But the tendency to form separate tribes often has a disastrous effect on communication. The physical setting in which work teams relate together can be designed to encourage integration between co-dependent teams.

What actions can be taken to overcome territorial barriers and develop constructive intergroup communication? Six practical steps are:

1   Bring departments and teams together physically and ensure that they are clear about the mission or driving force of the whole organization and know where their work fits into the overall plan.
2   Break down stereotypes by ensuring that people visit different departments and get to know members of other teams as individuals. This reduces superficial relationships but has to be deliberately encouraged. The natural tendency is to interact with existing contacts, rather than stretch out to new people.
3   Send departmental teams together on training programmes which enable people to recognize the difference between

'win–lose' relationships (where one side seeks to win at the expense of the other) and 'win–win' relationships (where both sides try to achieve their own goals and help the other side achieve theirs). Once people are aware of this distinction they should then examine their intergroup communication to try to change any win–lose relationships into win–win.

4   Bring managers or whole teams together to examine procedures for routine communication and simplify wherever possible. Use all available technological resources to overcome unhelpful geography.

5   Set up joint meetings for airing and resolving conflicts. Ensure that people come together to air differences of views. Devise mechanisms for positive resolution of conflict, and if necessary, arrange joint training in conflict resolution skills.

6   Create an environment where people can meet informally and develop a 'norm' of openness. Encourage people to be direct and non-political with each other. Informal and recreational outings are helpful. Admitting errors and weaknesses should be encouraged. The open approach cannot be successful unless senior managers demonstrate, by their own behaviour, that they believe in it.

These six steps are a programme for intergroup communication improvement. This is easier to sustain when departments are physically located close together. One manager put it this way: 'I've found, through experience, that it pays to locate people near to those with whom they are likely to have conflict. Most people put their purchasing department in a corner of the accounts area. I don't do that; I put the purchasing department next to the production managers as they are always fighting. Proximity builds mutual understanding.'

Usually, when space is allocated in a building, most concern is paid to providing adequate facilities for the competing demands. Status is often the prime concern and distracts the planners from giving full consideration to the communication aspects of their decisions. Managers are well advised to base team and departmental layout decisions on informal and formal communication needs.

Geography and the whole organization

The geographical spread of organizations brings severe communication problems. A large manufacturing company was in an expansionist mood in the 1970s and purchased a company in Italy which had great technical and marketing strength. The benefits of the acquisition were never realized. Top executives gave no thought to potential problems of communication across national boundaries at the time of purchase. Four years later the companies despaired of working together effectively. In fact, visitors to the head office were shown a three-inch thick file boldly labelled 'Unanswered telexes'.

Many large organizations have adopted a policy of geographical decentralization as they believed that monolithic and centrally controlled enterprises were demotivating, cumbersome and stunting of initiative. The benefits of breaking large organizations into physically separate and autonomous units include clearer accountability, improved motivation, more flexibility, easier industrial relations and less red tape. From many points of view 'small is beautiful'. Although communication within units improves in decentralized organizations there are new communication problems for the total organization. It becomes difficult for one unit to exploit areas of expertise in other units and economies of scale are lost. Some sites go their own way and undermine the overall management strategic concept. Solutions to these problems include an integrating role for headquarters staff, better corporate planning processes, and greatly improved management information systems.

Problems of organizational geography are not confined to commercial organizations. Many such difficulties were faced by the British Ministry of Defence during the Falklands War. One senior officer said at a press conference: 'The greatest problems are geographic – of course the 12,000 miles is a logistical problem but we can plan our way out of that. More intractable is the communication between specialists and field commanders. A specialist under a local commander will usually not be used effectively and yet if we try and control the specialists from London all co-ordination is lost. Frankly it is a problem that we don't know how to solve.'

Such problems of organizational communication are likely to become more acute in the next twenty years. Increasingly both business and service organizations are international in scope. Products are developed on a world-wide basis. A director of a company which has factories in fifty-one countries put it this way: 'If we fail to compete on a world level we will be eaten up. The answer is "world product management" but we have to solve the communication problems. It means a lot of people on airplanes but there's no other way to go.'

International communication involves cross-cultural issues. We tend to underestimate the difficulties of working with people who have a different language or culture. For example, some French-speaking Canadians dislike working with English speakers; the resources expended trying to make the European Common Market efficient are widely regarded as scandalous. Fortunately, not all projects which require multinational co-operation are doomed; the European Airbus was a successful enterprise which required an enormous amount of intercultural liaison. International teamwork is possible but difficult to establish. Management can break down barriers to effective co-operation by establishing social mechanisms which help to overcome cultural or geographical differences.

In conclusion, we need to realize that organizational geography is more significant than we generally assume. As people understand that co-ordination, integration and enjoyment is greatly influenced by the immediate physical setting, they take action to try to improve the situation. However, the opportunities for designing helpful geography are limited unless architects and planners specifically consider the human consequences of their decisions before the first brick has been laid.

Organizations thrive when they are like villages. Successful environments are human in scale with easy ways to communicate with others. It is important for people to feel a strong sense of identity. We can envisage greater integration as organizations become 'electronic villages' which link people by video, computer and telecommunication services. Those who design organizations need to learn that geography plays a central role in communication effectiveness.

Is unhelpful geography a blockage in your organization?

The following activities from the companion volume, *50 Activities for Unblocking Organizational Communication*, are especially relevant:

17 Workplace audit.
18 Communication within our building.

Downward flow

Being directive: people are told what they should know to play their part.

Mary Johnson supervises a team of social workers who have to cope with many problems. Battered wives, neglected children, infirm old people and poor housing are just a few of the daily pressures. The most difficult cases concern families with children at risk. In recent years the policy was to support, not supervise, such families and social workers were instructed to take an attitude of co-operation rather than surveillance. However, some children were terribly ill-treated and senior officials decided that the policy should be reversed. Social workers should be required to put the physical welfare of the child first. Mary failed to convey this vital change of emphasis to the members of her team, and a child died through neglect.

What went wrong? Mary did not effectively direct information downwards. The social workers simply did not understand what they should do. They carried on using old guidelines. Consequently, senior management's policies were not implemented and terrible consequences followed. The organization disintegrated because downward communication was defective.

The absence of effective downward communication creates a vacuum. People make up the rules for themselves and control their own behaviour. Such communication vacuums have a corrosive effect on morale. They encourage anarchy, suspicion and mistrust; people seek security, either taking initiatives for themselves, or turning to protective agencies, like trade unions, for support.

The downward flow of information can be an integrating force in organizations in five ways:

1   Direction and control – tells people what they must do: enabling management to direct and discipline the organization.
2   Informing – gives information to the individual which is needed for personal decision making.
3   Involvement – tells people what they want to know, so helping them feel part of the organization.
4   Giving meaning – enables people to perceive their work as part of a collective effort.
5   Flexibility – helps create the readiness for organizational change.

These are the motives for downward communication. This chapter considers the first, direction, in depth. The other four are dealt with elsewhere in this book. Specifically, informing is discussed in the chapter on 'Communication skills,' involvement in the chapter on 'Supportive teamwork,' giving meaning in the chapter on 'Compelling vision' and flexibility in the chapter on 'Persuasive management'.

Direction and control

From the managerial viewpoint, downward communication ensures that organizations are well directed. This is so important that management hierarchies are designed to cascade directives from the top to the bottom. Those at the apex have power, but need mechanisms to carry their values, policies, strategies and objectives downwards.

Direction implies control. A chief executive decides that all salesmen will wear white shirts and grey socks. A directive is issued, but is unlikely to be implemented unless the salesmen are controlled. Someone has to inspect their clothing and punish transgression. Control is a very important concept. In order to help us understand the relationship between direction and control I will discuss the three types of control in more depth.

The first method of control is 'action planning'. This requires those with authority to plan what actions are needed and others are expected to play their part. When several fire crews attend a straightforward incident, the firemen look to their chief for instructions. Only he has the information to direct operations. The firemen do what they are told, and integration is effected by a military-style chain of command.

Where the primary method of control is action planning, people need to know what should be done, what sequence to follow, how to perform the defined tasks and what to do if things go wrong. Downward communication, therefore, should ensure that the required behaviours are specified to ensure a high standard of achievement. An almost mechanical adherence to procedures is sought.

The second method is 'performance control', where those with authority determine what results are needed, give objectives and then measure performance. Actions are not planned, as people are allowed to find their own ways to get things done. To illustrate the point, consider the firemen again. Suppose that the incident is not straightforward and a team must enter the smoke-filled building to find the heart of the fire. The fire chief will pick an experienced crew and instruct them: 'Get to the seat of the fire and try to put it out'. The team sets off with this objective, but no preformed action plan. They take initiatives and develop action plans themselves in the light of circumstances. The fire chief monitors performance. Integration is effected by management by objectives.

Where the primary method is performance control, participants must understand the required end results of their efforts. They need to be sure about the boundaries of their authority, the resources available, how they will be measured, and the relative priorities of different objectives. Downward communication, therefore, should ensure that the required objectives are specified, but should leave action planning to responsible individuals or teams.

The third method of control is 'policy enforcement' – policies are laid down which specify how people should behave. Our fire chief may believe that there are some children trapped in the burning building. A newspaper reporter approaches him and asks: 'What are the names of the children?' The fire chief mentally checks section 13, paragraph 18(b) of the procedure manual and replies: 'I cannot give you any personal details until the next of kin have been informed'. This is the fire service policy and the chief operates within it. Integration is effected through standardized application of policies and principles.

Where the primary method of control is policy enforcement, people need to understand the policies, rules, guidelines and conditions which circumscribe their work. In addition, they need to be able to categorize situations so that the 'correct' stance is taken. Downward communication, therefore, should ensure that the meaning and the content of policies are understood, and practitioners are skilled at diagnosing when a particular policy is appropriate.

It is a principle of organization that action planning becomes less possible as unpredictability increases. The fire chief does not know what the crew will find as they work their way down smoke-filled corridors to the heart of the burning building. He could set an objective and establish policies, but not specify the actual behaviour required. Action planning provides the most comprehensive way to integrate the work of many people, but becomes counterproductive in uncertain situations.

Control is important to managers because their primary task is to decide what should be done and to ensure that the wanted results are achieved. Their basic decision is what form of control should they use – action planning and/or performance control and/or policy enforcement. Once this has been decided, the requirements for downward communication become clearer.

In small organizations downward communication for direction can be efficient but informal. It is easy for the boss to be in close contact with all employees without elaborate systems. However, large organizations cannot operate on this basis. They require formalized procedures for communicating downwards. The content of such communication goes beyond action plans, objectives and policies to deal with all aspects of organizational life.

There are four ways in which downward communication can take place in large organizations:

1   Line communication – information is systematically cascaded from top to bottom through the levels of the management hierarchy.

2   Communication to representatives of the workforce – information is given to workers' representatives, normally trade union officers, who transmit it through their own structure.

3   Mass communication – top management use the methods of mass communication, like newspapers, videos, presentations, notices etc. to contact all employees directly.

4   Training and indoctrination – structured instruction, courses, and other learning experiences are used to get across complex messages, to change attitudes and to inculcate skills.

These four methods of downward communication are not mutually exclusive.

Line communication

The first method, line communication, reinforces the managerial power structure. Action plans, objectives and policies and state of the nation messages are generated at the top and transmitted downwards, level by level, until everyone has received the information. Typical messages cover performance, new products, new orders and so on. Inevitably, such information is management-oriented.

Perhaps the world's leading consultancy in line communication, The Industrial Society in London, recommends a structured approach which it terms 'briefing groups'. Each manager is carefully trained to conduct periodic briefing meetings. The mechanisms for cascading information are made crystal clear. Briefing meetings are led by named individuals at specific times to a carefully designed format. Managers, however, add information specifically related to their own departments, so that messages are more likely to be relevant. The briefing group method helps management get its messages across reliably and predictably.

Although briefing groups include a mechanism to channel questions and reactions upwards, it is not consultative. There is no pretence at power sharing: briefing groups are a device for taking management's message downwards.

One point must be watched. Some downward communications, by their nature, tend to be mundane and boring. Who cares if the deputy marketing director's assistant has taken over responsibility for Borneo, or the three-part parts order form will have a six figure number from 17 March? Downward messages must be attuned to the needs of the receivers.

The information that people need and want is greatly affected by their immediate situation. The most pressing problem for a supermarket checkout operator may be the broken spring in his seat. The checkout operator wants to know: 'When will I get a new chair?' and the relative profitability of the stores in the group is of little immediate relevance. Indeed, he may become irate if managers communicate what concerns them and ignore what impacts on him.

What people want to know is almost impossible to predict. A seventeen-year-old boy whose preoccupation is keeping his hair the proper shade of electric blue has very different concerns from a thirty-year-old man with three young children and an ailing wife. One employee may want to know whether his company uses a research laboratory which experiments on animals, while another is anxious to calculate the probable returns on her pension if she goes to live in Tierra del Fuego in the year 2010. Downward communicators should study the needs and wants of those who receive the messages (see the chapter on 'Upward flow').

Students of line communication realize that a structured approach is only part of the story. The actual behaviour of senior managers is a powerful form of communication. Consider this example: a group of personnel managers watch video films from the Harvard Business School, which portray two Xerox executives living through a typical workday. The first executive is highly structured as he sets precise objectives and exercises firm control. The second gives every appearance of being a relaxed, laid-back and unstructured Californian who drifts around chatting for a large part of the day. Yet both men are equally successful. One executive adopts a formal communication style, for example, carefully scripting his presentations down to the exact instant when a new slide will appear. The second man is inspirational, magnetic, forceful and radiates concern with the quality of life.

What did the personnel managers learn as they discussed these video case studies? The leader's communication style sets the tone for the whole organization. Behaviour is communication in itself. As a member of the group remarked: 'The being of the man is the key. No matter how much you try to cover up your nature, it is bound to shine through.'

Roger Harrison, during a lecture, put it in this way:

> The potency of our behaviour as symbols is both good and bad news. It's good news because it doesn't require a capital investment – it's cost effective! It's bad news because every act we perform communicates, and therefore we communicate the truth about what we believe, take seriously, are determined or not determined to do, whether we are aware of it or not. Even when we don't know what we're communicating, the truth, or something like it, is getting across to those people who watch us more closely than we watch ourselves.

Line communication is less straightforward than it appears on paper. Managers start with good intentions, but fail to invest the necessary commitment. It's the organizational equivalent of jogging – everyone knows it's good for you, but the discipline is difficult to maintain. This means that managerial effort is needed. The process needs a champion, someone who wants it to happen and takes responsibility for its success.

Communication to workforce representatives

In most large organizations employees combine together to form an alternative protective power group, which may be a docile staff association or a fiercely aggressive trades union. The fact that counter-organizations have formed in every industrialized country demonstrates the real need for them. Workers' representatives have their own meetings and lines of communication. Also, they have an advantage: usually unions are trusted, whereas management is viewed much more warily.

In large organizations communication about the basic contract between management and labour may become a stylized encounter between the representatives of both sides.

Like the gladiators of old, representatives enter battle and their conclusions are binding. From the management viewpoint, this process has one great advantage – clarity. Once an agreement is made, there is no more debate. However, the existence of an alternative power structure with different aims is a potential threat to any organization. In fact, the concept of 'two sides' is a major communication blockage which is discussed further in the chapter on 'Lack of prejudice'.

It is rare to find a manager who unequivocally welcomes trades unions, although once they exist managers are well advised to build a deep level of understanding. A trade union which has the trust of its members can do much to help integrate the organization by supporting management. Management needs communication strategies which exploit the strengths of trade unions in pursuit of organizational goals. Workers' representatives are hard to fool, so a strategy of persuasion will only be effective if it is based on defensible arguments and a high level of mutual trust (see chapter on 'High trust').

Using workforce representatives as part of the downward communication process has its attractions. It removes a burden from management and simplifies the communication task. However, such a policy has serious inherent dangers. It strengthens workers' representatives ('information is power') and there can be no assurance that information will be faithfully communicated. On balance, therefore, management is well advised not to depend on communicating through representatives of the workforce.

Mass communication

We live in a society which bombards us with messages. Much creative effort has been invested in making mass-communication effective. A great deal is known about communicating complex information in persuasive and understandable ways. This means that managers have to communicate with a knowledgeable workforce. Almost everywhere today we see an enormous amount of communication: newspapers, television, radio, magazines, posters and so on. Most of these media have one thing in common: they are presented by professional people who understand the principles of effective mass-communication.

Organizations create much information. Most of which is conventionally expressed in a bureaucratic format. Information presented in this form is readily forgotten. Within three days, on average, people forget 80 per cent of what they read and 90 per cent of what they hear. However, if they both read and hear a message then about 45 per cent is recalled. There are two implications. First, maybe you ought to read this book out aloud to your children as a bedtime story! Secondly, to get their message across, managers have to acquire the skills of mass-communication.

The mass-communication methods used by managers include:

○ live presentations – which have immediacy and encourage group feeling
○ television films – can be carefully prepared and used flexibly
○ newspapers – can also be carefully prepared and are a permanent record, are usually regular and so open a channel for communication
○ poster campaigns – get across simple but powerful messages
○ community radio – tends to be background but persuasive
○ noticeboards – simple but flexible, especially useful for formal messages
○ books/manuals – enable complex information to be available in a permanent form.

Experienced managers emphasize that timing is extremely important. A premature message can alarm or backfire while tardy communication is irritating, impotent or counter-productive. The frequency of communication needs careful consideration. Excessive communication is wasteful and too infrequent communication breeds cynicism.

Mass-communication is sometimes subtle, especially when it is used as a mechanism for preparing people for a change. A major brewery in the United States planned to restructure its business. Some months in advance of the announcement of job losses, management allowed bad news to filter down as rumour. When the restructuring came, the workforce was psychologically prepared. As the personnel executive observed: 'The first thing that has to be done in implementing change is to open people's minds'.

In order to sustain high trust it is always important that employees are aware of the 'state of health' of the organization. This is vital when adversity strikes. When an organization goes into decline the reality of the situation is often denied. Surprise, fear, threat and assault on existing values are common emotional reactions to realizing that things are bad. Managers are likely to suffer from a more limited span of attention, decreased flexibility, and an unconscious desire to deny the truth of what is happening. Despite psychological difficulties, downward communication is crucial to recovery. A deep understanding of what needs to be done must be cascaded downwards, using the vehicles discussed in this chapter. A useful rule of thumb is: 'the more radical the decision, the more energy needs to go into communication'. In general, senior managers communicate too little, too late. This is especially true where powerful executives are deeply entrenched in the organization. They may become secretive, incapable of making decisions, only seeking counsel from flatterers and either virtually paralysed by fear or so full of their own importance that they fail to allow reality to touch them. Downward communication is wanted and needed by everyone. Wise managers communicate bad news but emphasize the positive benefits of taking the medicine.

Training and indoctrination

A constant flow of downward communication is a key to organizational performance. When such communication is too complex to be handled in briefing or short mass-communication exercises, the remedy is training. Although it is widely recognized that training is a 'good thing', few managers appear to realize its full potential as a primary technique for directing and integrating people in pursuit of managerial objectives. Here is an example. In one of the few detailed studies undertaken on this topic, the Technical Change Centre in London studied two multinational food manufacturing companies who introduced virtually identical new product lines. Company *A* gave 12,000 hours of training to twenty-six workers and began planning training before the contract to supply new machinery was negotiated. The training was energetic, well funded, carefully monitored and extensive. When the equipment was installed and functioning, the costs were 60 per cent less on indirect manning and 50 per cent less on direct manning, and the equipment ran about 30 per cent faster than its competitor's. Company *B* gave almost no formal training, preferring to rely on its workers' natural wits. It had enormous difficulties in utilizing the equipment, and its labour costs were approximately five times greater than those of its rival.

Training is the most elaborate form of downward communication but, like the other methods discussed in this chapter, it shapes behaviour in ways which meet managers' requirements. Although these paragraphs all read like a manipulative strategy, there is no choice: managers must use all the tools available to maintain integration.

Even well developed organizational systems become disintegrated because of weak links in the chain. Every manager and supervisor must be involved. The downward flow of information is tested at the level of manager and subordinate. The hierarchy is the primary integrating mechanism in organizations. Everyone working in an organization needs to know the answers to these questions:

What are my objectives?
What am I expected to do?
How do I decide what is important?
Am I efficient?
Am I effective?
Am I giving my boss the information he/she needs?
Am I supporting my boss?
How well do I relate to my staff?
How well do I develop my staff?
How well do I relate to others outside my department?
What are my strengths?
How can I build on them?
What are my development needs?
Can you give me constructive criticism?
What training would help me?

How will my job change in the future?
How does the organization view my career potential?
What should I do to prepare myself for job advancement?
On what basis will I be rewarded for my efforts and ability?

These questions are answered either explicitly or implicitly. In a sense the individual is being integrated; influenced to behave in 'constructive' ways.

Again this reads like a licence for manipulation but, in truth, we are being indoctrinated all the time. The difference is that managers can take charge of the process and inculcate values, standards, habits and attitudes which support organizational objectives. There is nothing new in this; the Jesuits have used these guidelines for centuries.

Planning downward communication

All four methods of downward communication are necessary, but managers often underestimate the amount of work needed for effective communication. An example from my consulting experience makes the point. The executives of Softec met for a three-day teambuilding event and wrote a detailed mission statement. This was to guide their work over the next few years in an increasingly competitive market.

The top team were excited as they met a few weeks later to consider how the new identity of the company should be communicated to the 600 employees. Initially their suggestions were pedestrian and then the personnel manager said: 'I propose that we tackle this like a military operation. The aim is for everyone to really understand the mission statement and consider what it means to them. We need newsletters, briefing groups, workshops, posters, videos and a lot of informal discussion. The executives in this room have to identify the opinion leaders in the business and persuade them. As a team we have to stand up and be counted. We want people to join actively – not to dismiss our plans as another piece of managerial rhetoric.'

This proposal made the group pause. Suddenly they realized that downward communication was an extensive exercise. One member commented: 'It sounds like a lot of work, but we have no options. We need the support of the majority to succeed.' In fact, this team planned a communication strategy using critical path analysis and later obtained the willing support of the workforce.

Downward communication in all its forms is an indispensable management tool. The chief executive of a street cleaning service said to me in a moment of candour: 'Every day I send people out to clean the streets. They have to put up with abuse, dogshit and a job that never gets done. Each cleaner would rather be sitting in a warm café drinking coffee. Something has to keep them at it. They need a measure of fear, a measure of reward and two measures of direction.'

In conclusion, there are ten questions which managers should ask themselves as they plan to communicate downwards:

1 *What* do we communicate?
2 *When* do we communicate?
3 *Why* are we communicating?
4 *Where* should communication take place?
5 *How* should communication be done?
6 *Who* is responsible for communicating?
7 What *skills* are needed by communicators?
8 What *processes* or procedures are needed?
9 What *values* underpin downward communication?
10 How can we get *feedback* on the efficiency of communication?

How managers use power without provoking revolution will be discussed in the next three chapters.

Is defective downward flow a blockage in your organization?

The following activities from the companion volume, *50 Activities for Unblocking Organizational Communication*, are especially relevant:

19 Gobbledegook.
20 Communicating care.
21 Understanding instructions.
22 Group briefing.

Sustaining a healthy community

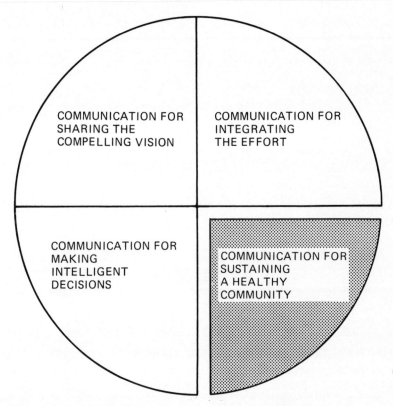

COMMUNICATION FOR
SHARING THE
COMPELLING VISION

COMMUNICATION FOR
INTEGRATING
THE EFFORT

COMMUNICATION FOR
MAKING
INTELLIGENT
DECISIONS

COMMUNICATION FOR
SUSTAINING
A HEALTHY
COMMUNITY

'People working for the organization, not against it.'

Definitions

Sustain – 'to keep (a person or community, the mind, spirit etc.) from failing or giving way'

Health – 'soundness of body; that condition in which its functions are discharged'

Community – 'common character; agreement; identity'

Shorter Oxford Dictionary

High trust

Being honourable: people trust those with power.

The ladies' lingerie business can be fickle. Some years ago, the producers of some of the world's most elegant negligées, brassières and camiknickers suffered in the economic recession. Orders declined as tasteful women went down-market in their quest for private luxury.

The exclusive lingerie firm was run by a shrewd and creative businesswoman but it suffered the same cash-flow anguish as any trader in difficult times. In Charles Dickens' novel *David Copperfield*, Mr Micawber pointed out that an annual income of twenty pounds is happiness if your annual expenditure is nineteen shillings and sixpence, but should your expenditure reach twenty pounds and sixpence, the result will be misery. This simple insight accurately summarized the predicament of the queen of underwear.

Then an interesting thing happened. The proprietor went to her staff and told them the facts of the situation, and they all decided to work for two weeks without any pay at all. Production continued, and the immediate crisis was weathered.

There have been countless other cases where managers have asked for support only to be greeted with total cynicism and a variety of obscene gestures. The proprietor of the lingerie firm enjoyed the trust of her workforce. That made all the difference.

Simply defined, trust is 'a belief that deeds will follow words and the other person will take your interest into account'. A message can be clear, understandable, accurate and relevant but if it is not trusted, the impact is destroyed. In fact, a message from an untrusted source may have exactly the opposite effect of that intended. The trustworthiness of a message is an important determinant of its effectiveness.

Why is trust so important in organizational life? For an explanation it is necessary to delve into the way that power is distributed. Most large organizations, even those in the Eastern Bloc, are not democratic. Those who wield great powers are owners and their representatives. Power comes from possession, not from persuasion. This means that those low down in organizations cannot control those who determine their well-being.

Despite the absence of democracy, almost all employees give their bosses a licence to manage. Most people accept the status quo and devote some effort towards corporate achievement. But, in the final analysis, the acceptance of the legitimacy of managerial power is dependent on those with high office being trusted. Should respect and trust break down, as happened politically in the Lebanon during the 1970s, then the right to manage is revoked.

Organizational health depends on willing acceptance of the legitimacy of management authority. Managers need people to support them and devote themselves to high performance. A productive 'contact', based on goodwill on both sides, is required between workers and organizations.

High trust is the outcome of a sound 'psychological contact' between leaders and led. It is proof that, despite the essentially undemocratic nature of almost all organizations, power is being wisely exercised. When managers are trusted they have permission to act with incisiveness and decisiveness. Self-surgery is accepted, even though it may require cutting off limbs to reshape the body.

High trust is an 'enabling force'. It enables organizational vitality to flow constructively, and so is an essential element in sustaining an energetic and flexible culture. The liberation of organizational vitality is central as routine operations become highly mechanized and automated.

Trust is a concept that has endured. It was admired by Socrates in ancient Greece, betrayed by Marcus Brutus in Rome, formed the ethic for the London Stock Exchange in the seventeenth century and is still widely regarded as the key ingredient of a successful marriage. The fact that trust has been prized in all communities for so many years indicates the enduring value of the principle. Trust is easy to recognize but difficult to define. To explore the concept further, it is helpful to consider those whom you trust. How did you come to acquire your belief in them?

The first criterion is honesty. We trust people who tell us the truth and give all the relevant information. The words of the oath in English courts elegantly summarize the principle. Witnesses are asked to 'tell the truth, the whole truth, and nothing but the truth'. Often in organizational life it is not possible to adhere fully to this principle, but people will accept that there are things they cannot know, welcoming the attitude expressed by one chief executive: 'I will tell you everything I can, and when there is something I can't tell you, then I'll tell you that'.

Some managers appear fearful of being honest, and their communications reflect this. In many organizations, workers look at the corporate newspaper and scathingly dismiss the contents as mere management propaganda. At some time they decided that their bosses were dishonest and continue to hold this view. Sometimes virtually all messages are treated as part of a management-inspired campaign to disadvantage the workforce. When investigated, there is often substance in such accusations. A deliberate façade or 'con-job' approach has been used by managers who naively believe that they can fool all of the people all of the time. Honesty means being honest even when it is embarrassing or unpalatable, and managers have to steel themselves for the demands that this principle entails.

The second criterion of trustworthiness is consistency. People become suspicious when messages change from one occasion to another. We all know the 'fair weather friend' – close and supportive whilst things are going well; only to disappear when adversity strikes. Willingness to tell the truth in good times and bad is essential for trust building. People have a deep wish to feel that those with power over them will stand firm despite difficulties.

I was once working as a consultant to a top team who wanted to develop their corporate identity. They insisted that the statement must reflect what actually happened, not an idealistic notion of what should happen. Early in the meeting the top team decided: 'We tell the truth to our workforce'. Later they admitted that they invested nothing in supporting the local community, but there was an outcry when I wrote on a flip chart: 'We will not support the local community'. The team said: 'It may be true, but we can't say it'. Of course, this went against the earlier decision to 'tell the truth'. For a person to be trustworthy their values have to be coherent, fitting together like pieces of the same jigsaw puzzle.

Like politicians, it is difficult for managers to be consistent. Circumstances change and managerial stances must alter. The need for greatest consistency is on matters of principle. Strategies change, but rules should endure.

The third criterion of trust is realism. We cannot trust those whose ideas are unrealistic and fanciful. People wisely validate what they hear by referring to their past experience. Managers are well advised to keep the scale of promises as low as possible to achieve their objective. In this way credibility can be more readily maintained.

The fourth criterion is follow-through. We all respect people who do what they say. When a promise is broken, trust is damaged. A marketing manager of an international company admitted: 'I've learnt an important lesson today. For months I have been making optimistic statements about a new product, but sales have been poor. Finally the figures have turned up. But I've burnt my boats. They've lost faith'.

The final criterion of trustworthiness is a belief that the other person will take all possible pains to act fairly and decently. We put our trust in others who act, wherever possible, in our best interest. This does not imply that those with power must take unqualified responsibility for the workforce. No one (except perhaps our parents) will give this degree of care. However, we want those with power over us always to act with compassion and respect our dignity.

It is worth pointing out that not all values can be respected. Even those which are humane may not engender support. A politician may be a kindly man but be derided as weak, whereas the street corner bully will be respected by some for his vicious sadism. Values which are respected over a long time are those which heighten the dignity of man and are pursued with vigour, in spite of inevitable challenges. From this point of view, management (like any use of power) is a moral responsibility. The moral element is probably best left unstated, but it should act as an unseen, guiding hand.

Being trusted is not altruistic. Managers reap the benefit as others perceive their integrity. This means having principles and sticking to them. Values establish guidelines for decisions on such matters as disclosure of information, honesty, truthfulness, fairness and consistency. Such values become powerful guides which shape managerial behaviour. They are so fundamental that they become part of the compelling vision which directs the organization.

Building trust

Trust is built when managers act from honourable motives. Bob Fisher became chief executive of a textile manufacturing group. He had a good track record as a senior operational manager, and wanted to become an industrialist of national stature. In his new role Bob had the right platform to be noticed. He became increasingly preoccupied with prestige, made speeches to many worthy bodies, sat on various committees and gave extensive interviews to the press. He bathed in the publicity, recognition and symbols of power. Yet this was not enough. Bob Fisher wanted to be remembered as a visionary and a strategist. He decided, with scant consultation with his colleagues, to move a large factory from a long-established location in a multiracial city to a new development area. The move was disastrous. Traditions of a loyal workforce were swept away. Trust was virtually destroyed. Nothing worked well, and no one cared enough to fix the myriad of problems.

A once profitable company became a loss-maker. Bob finally retired in ignominy and confided before he left:

> I made a serious error, quite unconsciously. I stopped thinking about business and started thinking about image. I allowed myself to be corrupted by power. I forgot to value the ordinary things in life and offended people by spoiling

that which they had worked to construct. They lost faith in me, and then everything went to pieces.

Sustaining trust requires recognition of human achievement. Many superb, worthwhile or valuable institutions have been swept away with scant regard for their value. Those institutions which provide for basic human needs like comfort, stimulation and consideration rarely change. So, the Turkish bath operates today very much as it did in Roman times and a western saloon in Arizona provides the same convivial atmosphere that cowboys enjoyed in the days of the gold rush. When such institutions are destroyed in a cavalier fashion, those involved realize that people with power have little respect for their history.

The management role always requires trust building. Roger Harrison described this well when he said: 'The individual is able to approach his or her role in the spirit of stewardship; leadership as a trust exercised for the benefit of all'.

Trust building forms the basis of a distinct management style which emphasizes authenticity rather than role playing. One of the leading proponents of humanistic psychology in the United States, Jack Gibb, conducted many training programmes to develop an understanding of trust. Gibb says the trust-building leader should not play false roles but become a full person by being assertive, warm, open, active, demanding to be heard, expressive of his own feelings and needs, and very much involved in decisions and processes in the group. In other words, the person who plays a role cannot be trusted. We have to be ourselves.

Gibb believes that any change, however significantly it may relieve the symptoms of distress, is dysfunctional if it does not move in the direction of increasing the trust level, openness, self-determination and interdependence. Trust encourages co-operating and care. It strengthens a bond between the individual and the organization.

Trust is built when people care for the well-being of others. We encounter numerous examples of selfish behaviour every day. A man drives too fast through a busy town; a woman empties her handbag on the pavement, whilst a dog-owner casually watches his pet soil a children's play area. Within organizations the same selfishness is common place; a cook fails to wash his hands before touching food and a senior manager stamps on a proposal without consideration or debate. Whenever self-interest is promoted at the expense of others, trust is damaged.

Building trust is a long process. There is a useful idea borrowed from the inspirational Eric Berne, whose work is discussed in the chapter on 'Supportive teamwork'. The notion is 'stamp collecting'. Do you recall how stores used to give Green Shield stamps which we would collect and stick in books? When a book was full of stamps it could be traded in for a prize. Well, trust building works in almost the same way. Each trustworthy act adds to the number of stamps in the giver's book. When the book is full, the holder of the book has gained sufficient trust for the prize.

A low level of trust, once established, is extremely difficult to remedy. Quite understandably, people dislike giving their trust a second time to someone who has abused them. Trust is built or destroyed day by day. Collective events have special value for trust building. The Japanese company AIWA established a factory in Wales in 1980. Founded on a principle of mutual trust by 1984 they were rapidly increasing output and required great commitment from their 150 employees to cope. One day, the wives of the Japanese managers, dressed for the occasion in kimonos, cooked and served a traditional Japanese lunch. The employees struggled with chopsticks, laughed with their bosses and enjoyed the occasion. The personnel manager said he was trying to build a 'factory identity'. Speeches were made and another step was taken in building a trusting workforce that is disposed to give management the 'benefit of the doubt'. Such events are positive ways in which trust is built.

Low levels of trust evoke defensive reactions. Subtle changes occur. People begin to plan not to fail, rather than planning to succeed. Disclosure is kept to a minimum. 'Red tape' (discussed further in 'Apt administration'), proliferates when trust is low. Much human energy is invested in building protective barriers. Image is promoted rather than authenticity. The organization is viewed as a hostile jungle in which people have to fight or flee.

It would be wrong to suggest that trust can be won without being trustworthy. People are unwise if they give trust easily.

One manager said: 'I learned something of great worth when I discovered that careful discrimination was needed to determine to whom and when to give my trust'. He elaborated: 'I've become less trusting. I've learnt that I have to be strategic when I give my trust. I used to be naive and gullible. Part of my personal development has been to learn to trust some people less and others more.'

High trust creates an environment in which people are prepared to be open about their concerns and weaknesses. At an executive meeting a finance director, overwhelmed by problems with a new computerized system, looked at his colleagues and said: 'I'm in the shit'. The chief executive replied: 'I'm glad you said that. It's good. Now we can deal with the problems. Twelve months ago, no one would have admitted that they had a problem. If anyone had intimated that they had a weakness then we would have torn them apart.'

In recent years senior managers have become more aware of the importance of maintaining a high trust climate. The phenomenal success of corporations like IBM, Nissan, Sony and Unilever, who emphasize business ethics, demonstrates that a foundation of good human relationships pays off. Policies, systems, conventions, procedures, rules and objectives ensure that people with power are accountable for putting the values into action.

Although it is said that 'principles cost money' the opposite can be true. A British manufacturer of advanced medical equipment developed a sophisticated cancer treatment which required reaction chambers to be manufactured in Germany. On calibration, excessive deviations of tolerance were discovered. The problems could only be discovered by sophisticated measuring equipment so users would not have detected the defects. But the manufacturer refused to supply inadequate products. Deliveries were stopped and the reluctant supplier was helped to find better ways of manufacturing the reaction chambers.

This principled decision cost many thousands of pounds but the company knew that inaccurate equipment would nullify any benefits for cancer patients. It took eighteen months to solve the technical problems. Hospitals and medical research centres heard the story through their sensitive grapevines and the company gained much trust. Initially the management had taken the decision on the basis of principles, saying, 'We will not supply inadequate equipment for treating cancer sufferers'. The managing director put it this way: 'If I cannot stand up in public and defend my decisions then I know that I am going wrong.' He added: 'I might be able to delude my customers but this would be unacceptable. I insist in being a trustworthy business.'

Managers can build trust by being:

○ constructive – seek to build and not damage
○ predictable – they do what they say they will do
○ conscious – decisions are taken with care to try to predict their probable outcomes
○ pragmatic – ways are found to meet commitments
○ defensible – individuals are prepared to stand by personal choices publicly.

Managers can take the following six steps to evaluate their trustworthiness:

1   Each manager writes his or her management principles and invites close colleagues to review the notes and discuss their reactions. Managers should repeat the exercise until a completely honest statement of principle has been prepared and then ask: 'Would you trust someone with these principles?'
2   Managers benefit from asking their subordinates whether they behave differently from stated principles. Such feedback helps clarify whether the manager is trustworthy.
3   Managers review written statements of corporate principles and compare these with their own beliefs. This enables any inconsistencies to be reviewed.
4   Senior managers undertake an additional exercise. They are invited to 'write a statement of management principles which you wish to see govern the part of the organization under your influence'. This is then discussed widely.
5   Managers are requested to find a mentor (older statesman) and ask what principles the more experienced manager finds work in practice.

6   Lastly, it is almost always useful for managers to visit particularly successful organizations and discuss their principles. These can be compared with the manager's own approach.

Being trustworthy is sometimes regarded as a soft and over-idealistic approach. The honourable people are outmanoeuvred and ravaged by unprincipled opponents. It is true that a commitment to being trustworthy can increase individual and collective vulnerability. It is necessary to be aggressive in defence of one's humanistic principles.

Trust is a topic which is particularly likely to be discussed in high-sounding but empty phrases. One manager, who had strong moral convictions, decided to put great emphasis on values. She insisted that a 'principle charter' was prepared and required a monthly 'principles audit'. The process became a charade. Other managers saw the monthly audit as an amusing diversion and they secretly called it 'Sunday School'. The motives were honourable but the process was unreal and ineffectual. As mentioned above, the deepest values should be like Victorian children – seen and not heard.

Principles are easy to espouse but difficult to apply. It is wise to be cautious about the written expression of values. In fact, there is a good case for arguing that a statement of values should be drawn from experience rather than from heady idealism.

In the final analysis, organizational trust is enhanced or diminished by the character of the people chosen to fill positions of power. If influence is in the hands of nincompoops, exploiters, egomaniacs or the indolent children of privileged people, the trustworthiness of management is diminished.

Is low trust a blockage in your organization?

The following activities from the companion volume, *50 Activities for Unblocking Organizational Communication*, are especially relevant:

23   Team openness.
24   Contracting for co-operation.
25   Avoiding groupthink.

Lack of prejudice

Being fair: no categories of people are disadvantaged.

In 1892 King Kojong of Korea and his wife, Queen Min, were invited to a tennis tournament at the British Legation. After watching for some time Queen Min was heard to remark: 'These Englishmen are becoming very hot. Why do they not have their servants do it?' The queen was expressing an attitude typical of her social class. Such differences in attitude may be charming, but there is a less innocent side; one group believes that another is inferior and we have the ugly phenomenon of 'prejudice'.

Prejudice is a set of attitudes which predisposes a person to think well or badly of an identifiable group. It is based on logically invalid generalizations which cannot be supported objectively. Unfortunately, prejudices are difficult to change.

Perhaps we become prejudiced because the world is too complex to understand directly. People simplify, categorize and evaluate; one race judges the other as weak and so on. For good or ill human beings react to their fellows as caricatures. Some of the worst excesses of human intolerance result from prejudices. Meaningless destruction feeds off bias, preconception and untested assumptions.

Clear examples of the corrosive effects of prejudice on human communication have been seen in South Africa and Northern Ireland. In these cases the unequal social structures became deeply resented and gnawed at the entrails of social order. Eventually, these communities became riddled with dissent. Exactly the same malaises afflict those organizations which support prejudice, bigotry and legitimized social exploitation.

Prejudice inhibits communication because it increases social distance and decreases humanness. This is particularly damaging because prejudice is often energized by aggression and hostility.

Moreover, people who are the victims of prejudice share a bond and are thereby strengthened as a group. They share common experiences and so have ready communication. The term 'brotherhood' conveys this sense of closeness. Such groups often seek to change the policies of those in power and sometimes preach revolution.

So deeply ingrained is prejudice that we must expect to see it in organizations. This can be an important consideration for managers. Prejudice undermines co-operation, provokes conflict and inhibits genuine communication. Unfortunately, since prejudices are both deep and unconscious, they are difficult to eliminate.

From an amoral viewpoint prejudice is not always immediately destructive. An organization based on social inequality may survive for hundreds of years with few ill-effects. Political systems like those in ancient Egypt, medieval Europe and the southern states of America before the abolition of slavery actually required organizations to be prejudiced. Such systems have a short-term advantage as they allow exploitation of valuable resources at low cost. It is not until disadvantaged groups begin to rebel that the stability of the community is undermined.

Those who strive to eliminate prejudice base their views either on pragmatism or ethics. They feel that an enduring and 'good' organization gives everyone the same basic rights. This may be done for selfless motives, to meet legal requirements, or because it is believed that an equal-opportunity employer gains in the long term through avoiding digging an almost bottomless pit of festering resentment.

There are many advantages, both practical and ethical, when managers strive to eradicate prejudice. Especially important is that ability and performance are seen to be the only two criteria by which people are judged. Relevant for the theme of this book, communication between groups is kept open, so that differences between people may be resolved through co-operative and rational processes.

Much of the discussion on prejudice reads like a soapbox sermon: pious but unrealistic. I enjoy being somewhat pompous, but nevertheless I cringe when I write such homilies. Yet the points are serious and down-to-earth. Anyone who doubts the importance of fighting prejudice should reflect on the fortunes of the police forces in multi-ethnic cities. Many police services have found it necessary to undertake major programmes to rid themselves of obvious prejudice. Training, indoctrination, discipline, instruction and leadership are all used to increase the probability that citizens will be treated equally. Unless the police are unprejudiced, communities are divided and violence is a constant possibility.

Clearly this topic has implications far beyond the scope of management. It would be possible to dwell on philosophical questions at length and gain little practical benefit. I will concentrate on what can be done to reduce the harmful effects of prejudice on organizational communication.

The first step is for managers to be aware where prejudice may occur. The most common prejudices deal with fundamentals like:

○ colour of skin
○ religion
○ racial origins
○ sex
○ age
○ social class or caste
○ work undertaken
○ country of origin
○ membership of a political group
○ style of dress and presentation
○ existence of any handicap or disability.

From a management point of view, these eleven categories can be related to 'disadvantaged groups' and to 'social class'.

Prejudice and disadvantaged groups

Many groups feel disadvantaged for one reason or another. To some extent the fashion of the age brings certain categories of people into prominence. At the time of writing we have great emphasis on racial and sexual inequality. Older people, homosexuals, environmentalists, handicapped people, anti-nuclear activists and minority religions are all claiming to be disadvantaged.

People from disadvantaged groups often feel deeply hurt by being treated as inferior. My aunt was very ill in hospital but decided not to lie in bed quietly whilst surgeons discussed her illness as if she were an inanimate thing. She later observed: 'They talked about me as if I was an idiot or unconscious. One day I had to say "Talk to me. I am a person."' In a small way, my aunt had become a victim of prejudice, as surgeons are likely to see their patients as technical problems rather than as human beings with emotions.

Perhaps the most obvious examples of prejudice are seen in relationships between the sexes. A female welder or production manager is constantly made aware of her sex. The stereotype of women as moody, passive, unreliable and emotionally unstable has little, if any, scientific validity. In a study of the health and performance records of a group of academically matched British civil servants carried out by Dr Rachel Jenkins, there were no differences found between men and women for such symptoms as anxiety, tearfulness, irritability or depression. The primary disadvantages of sexism are that goodwill is damaged and human potential is wasted.

Many disadvantaged groups eventually begin to protest. Senior managers usually see aggressive demands from disadvantaged groups as direct threats. The usual pattern is that managers are perceived as using their power to maintain a repressive system. Relationships tend to polarize and debate is conducted through slogans rather than rational debate.

Managers may take an initiative to reduce the causes of disadvantage; or they may be forced to examine such issues by external pressures. In either event, once managers have decided to take the matter seriously they must address the following questions:

Who are the disadvantaged group?
What, exactly, are their viewpoints?
What is our organization's policy towards such matters?

Is our past policy still right?
How radical a change is demanded (i.e. how much would it hurt us to concede)?
What would we gain by conceding?
How far are the disadvantaged group willing to compromise?
How much support does the disadvantaged group have?
Is their support likely to grow?
If we ignore it, will it go away?
Does management want to fight on this issue?
What is the best way to manage any change so that both the organization and the disadvantaged group win?

Such an analysis assists managers to determine their approach to disadvantaged groups. Leaders are well advised to take a long-term view on such matters. An expedient solution which may 'get us out of trouble today' can result in 'double trouble' in the future.

Prejudice and social class

Some observers argue that attitudes of people from different social classes are so different that almost all breakdowns in communication can be traced back to this fundamental cause. Karl Marx, in his sociological writings, forcefully described the effects of economic position on attitudes and communication. Even though we may not agree with Marx's conclusions, there was much wisdom in his analysis.

Social class is a reality. Attitudes, work practices, education, way of life, and even physical size are directly related to social class. To be precise, social class is too narrow a term for this discussion. Not all countries have identical approaches to stratifying their society. In India the Hindu caste system still governs many aspects of human relationships, while in Japan merit and tradition form the basis of social position. However, for western managers the term 'social class' is sufficient for our purposes.

Class differences are important to managers, even though they may not be fully aware of the many aspects of communication, relationship and decision making affected by them. Managers concerned with human motivation and industrial relations are deeply involved in social class. They experience the differences of interest and perception first hand.

Class prejudice works both ways. A friend of mine, now a director of a large company, reflected on the time when he worked as a labourer in a steel works. 'I used to get covered with muck and whenever I went to the front office I would despise the executives there. They were dressed in smart suits, looked clean and intelligent. I thought, "these aren't real men" and would have nothing to do with them. The irony is that now I go to work in a suit and if I'm not careful I think of labourers as dull and replaceable units of labour.'

To understand the effects of social class on communication we need two concepts: status symbols and stereotypes.

Status symbols

Status symbols are signs that we use to establish our place in the social hierarchy. Chickens establish a pecking order in the farmyard and people follow similar rituals. Everyone knows the symbols which mean something in his or her organization; it may be the quality of carpet on the floor, a place name in the front car park or that infamous key to the executive washroom. A friend of mine was appointed as a senior manager and was shown his new office, a large room with a sizeable alcove at one end. He looked at the alcove and thought 'This space will be ideal for storing my technical library'. Imagine his fury when he arrived on the first day to find a workman boarding up the alcove. He was told: 'Managers of your grade are entitled to no more than 150 square feet of space. With the alcove it comes to 163 square feet, so the alcove has to go.'

Status symbols are not easily eradicated. At one time I was involved in determining the company car policy for a large human-relations consulting organization. In the interests of reducing differences between levels I convinced the executive committee that consultants and senior consultants should be issued with identical cars. This was done, but two years later senior consultants formed a pressure group and obtained larger cars with lots of gadgets. The lure of status was stronger than a belief in equality.

Status symbols can be positive or negative. On the beneficial side some people are motivated by a drive to acquire the trappings of prestige, and easily identifiable symbols reinforce the existing authority structure. The negative outcomes are that status symbols encourage differences, thereby interfering with open communication and undermining the spirit of unity which is such a valuable motivational resource. Japanese companies, when setting up factories in Europe or the USA, make it one of their first tasks to eliminate obvious differences between status levels.

Management must use some form of hierarchical organization; so differences in status are essential. However, they can choose whether to widen or narrow the gap. Senior managers should be aware that their explicit and implicit policy on status symbols has a profound effect on the communication patterns within the organization.

Stereotypes

The second useful concept is stereotypes. These are simplified views formed about other people and then acted upon. Stereotypes touch every aspect of our lives, as these examples illustrate:

○ redheads are more emotional than brunettes
○ management cannot be trusted
○ women don't have what it takes to handle power
○ blacks are never on time
○ German products are always superior.

The extent to which stereotyping influences our thinking is well known to advertising specialists who spend millions attempting to create favourable images of corporations and products. Today politicians are marketed like a new variety of cheesecake. Once people form a stereotype they behave as if their belief was true and resist changing it.

Communication in organizations is affected by stereotypes; usually for the worse. This is most harmful when we look at the relationships between workers and management. One manager described his workforce as 'units of labour to be used to best advantage, but much more trouble than a robot because they won't do what they're told'. A shopfloor worker from the same factory, with a gift for rhetoric, described managers as 'soulless exploiters whose word cannot be trusted and whose only desire is to break the spirit of the working class'. Where such stereotyped attitudes exist there is little hope of open communication.

It would be convenient if stereotyped viewpoints could be easily eliminated. However, this is not possible. In fact, stereotypes can sometimes be strengthened by 'mutual understanding sessions' that are intended to reduce them. There is no easy remedy for racial, religious or class stereotypes, but action can be taken to create a climate which helps to confront the issues involved. People cannot be made to give up their stereotypes but they can be helped to test their views by exposing them to objective assessment. There is some evidence that it is possible to reduce stereotyping over a long period. For example, in one study 62 per cent of American servicemen who had not worked with blacks thought that they would dislike this very much, whereas a similar group who had worked with blacks showed that only 7 per cent felt this way (see A. M. Rose, *Studies in the Reduction of Prejudice*, American Council on Race Relations, Washington 1947).

Open communication between members of different social classes can be built by deliberate management action. When the Mars company set up a new factory in Europe they took active steps to prevent managers from becoming an inward-looking clan. All offices used an open-plan layout, only one cafeteria was built and relationships operated on first-name terms. Mars encouraged grievances to be aired and promoted an open style of management. Selection criteria for new managers emphasized skills in handling group discussions. Within Mars it was made almost impossible for managers to remain aloof and separate. Their tradition of open relationships laid the foundation for communication without interference from historic social class stereotypes.

Although social class is detectable in North America and European countries it is in British companies that it has been a serious barrier to communication. But things are changing. In

1980, only 40 per cent of a representative sample of companies had a canteen where managers and workers ate the same food. By 1986 the figure had risen to 60 per cent (*25th Survey of Catering*, Industrial Society, London 1986). Once people eat together there is a possibility that stereotyping will decrease.

Union management relationships have often been based upon perceptions of the 'other side' as self-seeking, manipulative exploiters, liars and cheats. However, this does not have to be the case. When the United Biscuits company in England announced that it was considering closing a factory a fascinating event in industrial relations occurred. The company provided very detailed commercial arguments as to the reasons why a closedown was necessary. Local trade unions met to consider their reaction. The proposal meant that another 1800 people would be jobless in a city already scarred by massive unemployment. The first response of workers' representatives was to consider all kinds of militant and defensive action. Should they occupy the factory or slow down production as a visible demonstration of their anger?

Interestingly, such negative actions were abandoned and the trade unions funded a study into the possible commercial revitalization of the factory. This was conducted by a group of bemused management consultants surprised to have a commission from 'the other side'. The company adopted an open approach; they provided all relevant statistical information for the consultants to do a thorough study. James Dunlop, the factory director, said on television: 'We decided to be totally open. Nothing could be gained by taking a high-handed or secretive attitude'. The trade union recovery plan was professionally presented with well considered commercial arguments. The board of directors of this multinational company took the matter very seriously, realizing that they included a proposal to reduce the workforce by about one-third. This was an almost unprecedented willingness to conduct essential but painful self-surgery.

The trade unions, the workforce and management struggled to find a viable continuing commercial role for the factory and it became clear that a breakthrough had occurred in industrial relations. The traditional patterns of communication based on social-class-based stereotypes were swept away by a concern to attain a shared goal. The company did much to encourage such an attitude by its directness, preparedness to talk, and willingness to give adequate time for a genuine debate. The trade unions played a constructive role through their initiative to engage professional help, recognition of the strengths of commercial arguments, and engaging in serious dialogue. Perhaps the most striking observation was made by a factory worker: 'Whatever way the decision goes, I feel that the fight has been worth it. We see management's point of view; they see ours. You can't ask for more than that.'

In the event, the factory closed but the experience emphasizes how an approach to communication which goes beyond stereotypes lays a foundation for co-operation. Without this there is a wide gulf between groups and negative, defensive, mutually destructive behaviour.

Stereotyping can be reduced by the following actions:

1   Publish a totally honest and 'bullshit-free' policy statement which lays down the stance that the organization takes to industrial relations, disadvantaged groups and prejudice.
2   Use training and self-survey techniques to raise conscious-ness about the existence of stereotypes and encourage people to consider their beliefs rationally.
3   Use mass-media presentations to fight against prejudice; there is evidence that people are influenced by convincing films, video tapes etc.
4   Hold 'get to know each other' sessions in which people are helped to understand the history, language, ideas of other groups.
5   Develop programmes to help people really experience the environment of others (for example; getting managers to work on the shopfloor and production workers to visit customers etc.).
6   Ensure that managers make personal contact with people of every level (by doing away with the symbols of superiority).
7   Provide opportunities for people to meet informally.

These actions look bland when merely set out on the printed page. The ideas must be energized to fight against prejudice. This can be done. When a new Nissan factory was opened in northern England a documentary film was made to demonstrate the management style. Television viewers saw diminutive Japanese executives, sitting behind large glasses of beer, talking to new employees in carefully structured get-to-know-you sessions. Everyone present was wearing an identical uniform. Dour and hard local workers, conditioned to be cynical towards the bosses through a century of industrial relations animosity, showed surprising positiveness. They were affectionate towards their new Japanese masters whose family-style workplace was winning new friends. Nissan had fought prejudice and won.

The message is simple. Prejudice is an enemy of open communication. It must be identified, confronted and vanquished. Then managers must watch to see that this insidious malaise does not reoccur in some different form.

Is prejudice a blockage in your organization?

The following activities from the companion volume, *50 Activities for Unblocking Organizational Communication*, are especially relevant:

26   Tribal.
27   Social class stereotypes.
28   Are we a prejudiced employer?

Supportive teamwork
Being co-operative: people work well together.

Radox Electron is an Australian company employing nearly five hundred people making electronic defence equipment. Three years ago they faced daunting business problems – profits were down and there were serious delays in the development of new products. The chief executive told an emergency meeting of senior managers: 'We're deep in it. Some decisive action has to be taken. I want to know what is wrong, and I want it straight.' Their discussion lasted until 2 a.m. The causes of the business crisis were described this way: 'We blew it. We've had our heads in the sand. The senior managers ought to have worked as a team. But there has been no collective support. Instead we bitched and moaned and fought each other.'

Each Radox executive had perceived his chief responsibility as running his own department to the highest standards. There was little concern for the 'collective good'. The top team, which should have integrated the specialist departments, functioned instead as a delegate committee. The chief executive loved invention and globetrotting, but failed to act as team leader. The lack of teamwork cascaded down through the company. Important issues became 'someone else's problem'. There was a general lack of support, which meant that serious problems were ignored.

'Support' is the key concept. It occurs when people are committed to helping others to do well, not weakening them by undermining their self-respect. Confrontation, challenge, directness and demand can all be helpful. Support is a mixture of caring, confidence, guidance and optimism. It is wrong to consider support as a namby-pamby notion only appropriate in the nursery.

From psychologists we learn that support is essential for wellbeing. People need warmth, closeness and encouragement. There is ample evidence that without emotional support, people deteriorate and become twisted, withdrawn and negative. There is a deep human need to be recognized, and treated as a valued individual.

How is support given? Those who look at behaviour from anthropological or biological viewpoints consider man to be an animal who thrives in 'hunting bands'. Small groups succeed in the face of adversity when the same individuals alone would be demoralized and ineffective. For many thousands of years stone-age man hunted in small groups. The modern organizational equivalent of the hunting band is work teams, which develop from top to bottom in organizations. Support is the foundation of team effectiveness. It provides the ephemeral quality – goodwill – which enables managers to drive towards output objectives.

Teams are 'the most powerful tools known to man', They are the building blocks of organizations. Teams do not arise spontaneously; they are fashioned painstakingly from a collection of disparate individuals. Once built, teams can sustain high morale, solve complex problems and integrate the work of specialists.

So far this book has considered communication as a requirement of systems. This may mean little to the individual. Teamwork promotes communication at the 'micro level'. It touches everyone. It is the means by which people find their places in the whole. This chapter examines aspects of teamwork which promote support, and discusses the process of encouraging support through teambuilding. The illustrations concern management teams, although the same principles can be applied to all work groups.

Respect for difference

Support requires that we respect others, despite the differences between us. Consider this example. At one time I was consultant to the top scientific team of Baltech Inc., a company with a worldwide reputation for making scientific balances. For many years the company was led by dedicated engineers who insisted on technical excellence. In 1983 Clint Johnson was appointed as chief executive by the retiring founder of the company. Clint was a go-ahead executive with an MBA degree and ten years' sparkling achievement in marketing. He set about changing the company, saying: 'Baltech has a distinguished history, but must change. We've been engineering driven and must become market led. I want to transform the culture of the business.'

Clint set about rebuilding the top management structure. Highly regarded engineers found themselves replaced by eager young marketeers. One shrewd observer remarked: 'He's surrounding himself with clones. It's a dangerous formula.' It was apparent that the new chief executive only listened to those who thought as he did.

The company began to suffer. Quality deteriorated and the reputation for excellence was lost. Baltech's high-priced balances came to be regarded as inferior to standard products. Clint Johnson poured resources into an abortive project to enter the schools market for laboratory equipment. Within two years the company was on the verge of bankruptcy.

What had gone wrong? There was no shortage of commitment or talent. The main cause of the business collapse was that the chief executive failed to respect the different contributions that people could make. What I did was to survey the characteristics of Clint's top team using a questionnaire from the companion volume (activity 31). This confirmed the suspicion that the team was biased towards action and lacked engineering technical expertise and critical objectivity. When I discussed the results of the survey with Clint Johnson he candidly admitted: 'I failed because I derided everyone who did not think like me. I dominated rather than led.'

A supportive team thrives on respecting differences between people. Over recent years we have learned from the work of Meredith Belbin, Richard Boyatzis and Charles Margerison that it is possible to define the different roles of team members.

In fact, ten distinct team roles can be identified. Let us briefly review these in relation to the Baltech case.

1 Process manager

The process manager channels human resources to get things done. This involves forming teams, identifying people's strengths, setting objectives, structuring meetings, clarifying issues, allocating roles and maintaining momentum. The process manager draws out the best from people and has the skills of a good chairman. This is a role Clint Johnson should have played, but failed to.

2 Concept developer

The concept developer ensures that ideas are properly developed and evaluated. He or she does this by taking ideas and building on them, testing for validity, visualizing the potential impact of different courses of action, seeing possibilities and transforming ideas into practical proposals. The concept developer thrives on complex problems and enjoys challenges; the key skills brought to the team are vision, imagination, ingenuity, precise logical thinking and understanding. Clint Johnson's team had several people capable of playing this role, but they were all marketing-biased.

3 Radical

The radical contributes unexpected perspectives by considering problems from unusual viewpoints, seeing new possibilities, adopting unconventional approaches, generating insights and producing novel proposals. Radicals look afresh at reality and seek to understand anew. They refuse to accept traditional wisdom. The radical may be described as the maverick of the group. Clint Johnson played this role himself – probably his big mistake!

4 Harmonizer

The harmonizer builds morale by being relationships-oriented:

supporting, encouraging, understanding, being sociable and resolving conflicts. The harmonizer believes that efficiency is based on good human relationships. By building and maintaining morale, the harmonizer creates the preconditions for commitment, co-operation and performance. The harmonizer tries to ensure that team members enjoy each other's company and feel that they are gaining something valuable from their membership. This analysis of the Baltech top team revealed that no one played this role.

5 Technical expert

The technical expert contributes specialized information, distinctive knowledge or expertise from an expert, professional or craft viewpoint. The technical expert may be an accountant, marketing specialist, corporate planner, personnel specialist and so on. The technical expert contributes as a representative of an expertise, and may remain silent until a matter relevant to his or her specialization is raised. Technical experts are partisan but their advice is most important. Only the expert may know enough to give an informed opinion on a particular question. The engineering technical experts in Baltech had been removed from the top team.

6 Output driver

The output driver drives to ensure that jobs get done. This requires setting targets, delivering products, meeting objectives, completing actions and finishing tasks. Performance is valued for its own sake. There is a strong commitment to quality. They are responsive to time limits. The output driver may be intolerant of error, somewhat inflexible, and autocratic. They are the ones who are always checking to see whether things could go wrong at the last moment. The school laboratory equipment divisional manager played this role in the Baltech team.

7 Critic

The critic confronts the team with objective observations and carefully weighed opinions to assist in decision making. Critics stand back, judge what is going on, consider possibilities, look for possible pitfalls, sound notes of caution, question proposals and challenge ideas. Critics are not predisposed to be either negative or positive; they desire to be objective. If they are able and experienced, their critique contributes that most valuable element, wisdom. They are sceptical, decisive, accurate, stable contributors. This role was absent in the Baltech top team.

8 Co-operator

The co-operator is a diligent observer who actively assists the team in whatever ways are needed. He or she fills gaps by helping, adopting co-operative attitudes, being prepared to work hard and being adaptable. The true co-operator is a 'jack of all trades'. The role requires high observation skills, generosity, enthusiasm, lack of concern for protocol, and a breadth of capabilities. This role was absent in the Baltech top team.

9 Politician

The politician shapes the team's collective viewpoints by being opinionated, results-oriented, high in influence, building alliances, guiding others, being power conscious and persuasive. The politician acts like a magnet on iron filings, pulling everyone in the same direction. He or she feels that they know the right thing to do, and deliberately tries to influence other people. Clint Johnson played this role in the Baltech top team.

10 Promoter

The promoter links the team to others by being outgoing, sociable, building relationships, investigating resources, sensing out ideas and possibilities. They are 'fixers' and enable things to get done. The promoter deliberately gathers useful contacts, and makes connections outside the team. The role suits outgoing people who readily make friendships. The promoter is a salesman on the part of the team, sometimes acting as a bridge. The promoter can be something of a gadfly, moving easily from one situation to another and never seeing things through. Several of the members of the top team in Baltech could play this role.

What are we to learn from this analysis? Each of these ten roles was necessary to the top team of Baltech, but Johnson failed to respect the strengths that people different from himself could bring. He constructed an unbalanced team that failed to represent the company's capability. Despite working fourteen hours each day, the top team ruined a splendid business. Supportive teamwork requires a balanced team construction.

Honest dealing

There is a second cause of unsupportive teamwork which can destroy even well-balanced teams – 'dishonest dealing'. The principle is best explained by an example.

Patrick Rufford was an executive in a large local government organization, responsible for all district services. He was a short man who gloried in being aggressive and decisive, never forgetting that he had more power and influence than most. His team enjoyed disliking him. He would appear benign and supportive but would swoop with almost sadistic glee when someone made a mistake. Patrick was a fascinating study; he changed his image to suit the audience like an accomplished actor. To his bosses he appeared positive and caring, but his subordinates went in fear. One of his staff said: 'He's like a vampire. When he's got someone on the floor, belly up and begging for mercy, then he'll get stronger and boot them harder. What's worse is that it seems to do him good!'

Rufford's team was responsible for the River Don which ran through their area. As flooding was a distinct possibility it was decided to construct an expensive flood prevention system. A technically innovative scheme was devised and Rufford was given overall charge of the project with tight deadlines for completion. However, when the construction was half completed, serious civil engineering problems occurred. The geological structure of the river banks proved to be weaker than surveys indicated. Team members hid the problems from Rufford. One said later: 'Although we felt like naughty schoolboys the fact is we lied and deceived. We were frightened to expose ourselves to ridicule and humiliation.' Eventually a journalist from the local newspaper heard a whisper of a scandal, discovered the facts and exposed the crisis. Patrick Rufford first realized that there was a serious problem when he read the front-page newspaper report.

A study of this case gives us an interesting new perspective on the topic of supportive teamwork. A careful analysis showed that the fault did not lie with a failure of capability or procedures; rather the problems arose because the staff failed to support their manager. All of Patrick Rufford's staff knew that they should honestly report snags and setbacks, yet they chose to deceive and hide.

This is not unusual. People frequently act according to how they feel and their behaviour may seem totally illogical to an outsider. A study of supportive teamwork must take into account such non-rational factors which affect the quality of human relationships.

The matter was serious, and Jane Goodfield, a management consultant, was asked to help. She looked at Patrick Rufford's team to try to understand what had gone wrong. It became apparent that Rufford behaved in a crass authoritarian manner. The members of his team reacted like a group of youngsters to a critical and punishing parent. Even the civil engineers admitted that they behaved like naughty children. The local journalist who exposed the scandal dealt with objective facts, so could be said to be behaving in an 'adult' manner.

Jane Goodfield realized that honest dealing was seriously lacking. She decided to try to help Patrick Rufford by explaining how team communication had failed. So, at a private coaching session, she summarized the results of her confidential interviews with each team member. As she talked, Rufford's reactions played across his face. At first he went red with anger, and then he looked crestfallen, slumping back in his chair. Finally the colour drained from his cheeks and he began to show all the signs of fear.

At the end of her summary she turned to Rufford and said: 'Perhaps it's time you talked about this. I'm ready to listen, and to help if I can.' Rufford said: 'This is very difficult for me. A lot has gone wrong, but I must confess that I don't really understand the problem. What am I doing that's so destructive?'

Jane Goodfield said: 'A good way of understanding why your interaction with others has been flawed is to examine, in depth, the kinds of transactions you have with your team. Some formal psychological theory might help you to understand better. May I give you a short lecture?' Patrick Rufford nodded and sat back in his chair.

A Canadian psychotherapist called Eric Berne developed a theory of psychology based on a careful study of the ways in which people inter-related. He called the approach 'transactional analysis'.

I think that transactional analysis can give you some useful insights into your relationship with your team. Berne's most fundamental observation was that although people may think that they behave consistently, in reality they don't. All of your team members noticed this. Sometimes you behaved like one person and then switched your whole approach and behaved like someone completely different. This happened in an instant. When we carefully analyse human behaviour it becomes clear that our state of being, which we call an ego state, can vary dramatically from moment to moment. The signs that a change in ego state has taken place can be seen in our facial expressions, posture, choice of words and ways that we speak.

Transactional analysis tells us that there are three basic ego states called 'parent', 'adult' and 'child'. Each has been given a special definition. To understand what went wrong in your team it will be useful if I describe each ego state in some detail.

We'll start with the parent ego state. This begins to develop when we are young children, watching and reacting to our parents and other influential people. Through the eyes of a child we see the power of the parent and absorb into ourselves their mannerisms, standards, judgements and prejudices. In later life we sometimes replay our recollection of the behaviour of our parents, down to the tone of voice and the choice of words. It's as though a child records on video tape inside his head how he sees his parents and, although the pictures are distorted by immature eyes, these video films are stored throughout life ready to be replayed when the right buttons are pressed.

Sometimes our parent ego state is authoritarian, critical and harsh, but this is not always so; we may also nurture others. But it is the critical side of the parent ego state that undermines supportive teamwork. I think that this was happening in your team. The use of the critical parent ego state tends to result in problems being ignored, and actions tending to follow established rules even though the actual situation may require something quite different. There is usually strong defence of tradition, unwillingness to consider fresh ideas, and creativity is stifled. Subordinates feel judged and they 'close up', and the truth is often kept from the boss.

At this point Rufford interrupted. 'This is ringing a lot of bells for me. When I get anxious, I can see myself behaving as my father did when I was a small boy and came home covered in mud. I never thought to connect it with my parents before.'

Jane Goodfield smiled. 'There are lots of lessons about communication in transactional analysis', she said, 'but it's not all bad. Let me tell you about a more constructive ego state.

The adult ego state develops gradually in childhood and grows to maturity in later life. It is that part of ourselves that deals with the world in a logical and rational manner. Collecting facts, weighing opinions, relating ideas and coming to reasonable conclusions are all functions of the adult ego state. In this ego state the person behaves as a computer; everything is based upon the best available data and logical assumptions are drawn. The adult is a very valuable tool. Many people have to deliberately rein in their non-rational responses and put their adult in charge.

In the adult ego state the person tends to think in diagrams and structures, so it is possible to see several points of view at the same time. This would have benefited teamwork in your group, as feelings would not have been allowed to interfere with data gathering and assessment processes.

The rational processes of the adult are invaluable tools to supportive teamwork as they permit clear identification of problems, statement of goals and objectives, systematic information collection, thorough evaluation of options, careful planning, impartial evaluation of results, willingness to respect the views of others, capacity to handle complex situations and a 'clinical' capacity to handle 'nasty' tasks.'

Rufford nodded. 'I can see that there wasn't enough adult in my style. When things got tough I pushed, rather than listened. I was far too much in my parent ego state.'

Jane Goodfield replied: 'It looks that way to me as well, but you weren't the only one acting on non-rational impulses. Think about how your team reacted. In order to explain the process, I have to talk about the child ego state.

As the saying goes, 'children will be children'. We usually think of childhood as a brief period followed by 'growing up'. However, we retain our 'child' throughout life. The child ego state may be inhibited but it never disappears. Children are spontaneous, joyful, sad, frustrated, demanding, angry or loving, and they communicate how they feel in an instant. Children learn to manipulate people and situations to suit their needs, but are made to comply, often rebelliously, with the directives of others.

A person in the child ego state behaves as they did in the first few years of their lives. They move, talk, sit, laugh and react as they did all those years ago. Their thoughts, likes, dislikes and perceptions will be those they had as children. Many of your team members told me that they felt like children in your presence. They said that they hid things from you like a group of five-year-olds.

The destructive and manipulative side of the child ego state is hazardous in several ways. People become excessively excited and over-optimistic, they become irrationally distressed or disheartened, actions are taken impulsively, data are ignored, difficulties are taken personally, and debates degenerate into childish arguments.'

Patrick Rufford sat thinking. Eventually he said: 'It needs a lot of self-analysis. Tell me what you think went wrong.'

Jane Goodfield hesitated, and then answered: 'The lack of

team support was caused by you operating largely from the critical parent ego state, whilst your staff reacted from their child ego state.

The people in your team would often behave in ways that led to predictable end results. Often the motives were hazy and the payoff minimal, but the pattern was clear. Deep needs were fulfilled as subconscious intentions were played out. These psychological stratagems are *games*. They are almost always destructive to supportive teamwork.

Every game has a purpose; it fulfils the gameplayer's desires and proves yet again that the person's view of life is correct. The feelings of satisfaction may appear perverse, but they are real. The game justifies the individual's stance and so brings some stability to psychological life.

Here is an example of a game which I overheard recently – not in your department, incidentally – called 'Why Don't You – Yes But'. You will see how a manager, Tom, tries to give support by making suggestions, but is thwarted by a colleague, Bill.

Tom: 'It seems to me that you have insufficient resources to complete the project. Why don't you discuss the problem with personnel?' Bill: 'Yes, but personnel never help; they're not given sufficient discretion.' Tom: 'Why don't you tackle the problem by writing a detailed report to the co-ordination committee?' Bill: 'Yes, but it's so political that they just won't listen to reason.' Tom: 'Well another suggestion is to take the matter to our boss. Why don't you see her today?' Bill: 'Yes, but I've tried that and she's under tremendous pressure to cut costs, so no joy.' Tom: 'Sometimes a detailed study helps.' Bill is stubborn: 'Yes, but I have no resources for a study; you can never get anything done properly around here.'

You can see how it goes on. This game ends with both feeling irritated but justified in their positions. Tom feels that he has tried to be supportive and Bill feels he has listened, considered (up to a point), and come to the conclusion that nothing constructive can be done. So, when the project goes wrong, both Tom and Bill will be able to feel fully satisfied that they did everything possible.

Most games are harmful to teamwork because they reduce openness, stunt relationships and justify passive or destructive stances. They were frequent in your team. Games undermine the quality of human support and sabotage thoughtful systems and procedures. However, it takes two to play a game and obviously, without collusion, the game cannot be played.

Games are subtle but powerful ways for team members to maintain their own integrity through defence or attack. There are only two remedies with a chance of success: first, it helps for teams to learn to recognize games. Secondly, team leaders can set the tone by demonstrating that 'the way to get on around here is to play it straight'. This is what I think that you might need to do in future.

Reflecting on the Patrick Rufford case study provokes the question: 'Can anything be done to prevent such destructive encounters?' Simply describing team interaction as Jane Goodfield did, using transactional analysis concepts, seems to help. Much behaviour takes place below the level of consciousness. Once a team develops the ability to recognize ego states a valuable tool is acquired. Traps for the unwary are detected in advance as trained observers have more capacity to respond in effective ways. From a team support point of view the most common problem is that leaders take on the role of critical parent. Team members respond from their child ego state, perhaps with docile compliance or, more destructively, with crafty rebellion. The resulting communication blockages destroy the possibility of mutual support. They can be immensely expensive and time wasting.

Supportive teams develop their capability under good leadership, but are often helped by a deliberate teambuilding process. Teambuilding hastens the development of respect for difference and promotes honest dealing.

Teams are ready for teambuilding when:

○ the leader wishes to use a team approach
○ the group has objectives which require them to work together

○ they possess the basic attitudes and skills needed for team working.

In a teambuilding session each team member is asked to evaluate openly how the team is operating. The focus is on team support. Inevitably shortcomings are exposed, so the team leader is in a vulnerable position. It takes leadership courage to begin teambuilding.

Some teams use the services of a teambuilding consultant. The consultant's assignment is to help the team to confront how it operates at present and build a supportive climate. This means identifying blockages to effectiveness, specifying the role the team should play, reviewing current process and planning how to improve. The consultant methodically collects data on such matters as values of the team, mission in the organization, goal clarity and commitment, relationships and accountability, decision-making processes, communication, leadership style, rewards, openness and trust, co-operation and competition, relationships with other teams, and practical issues of the moment which need to be addressed. The data are categorized and presented to the team manager in a private coaching session. A teambuilding event is held away from the office. A country hotel is ideal. Usually, such sessions begin after work one evening and conclude at dinner time on the third day. This gives two complete days of work, necessary for an adequate review of team functioning.

Teambuilding encourages supportiveness, but does not create it. There is a personal choice – people have to decide whether to opt in or not. Once everyone has signed up the team develops. Each member needs to gain from membership.

I began this chapter by reviewing the misfortunes of Radox Electron. There is a happy ending to the story. The top team underwent a teambuilding process. Before, none of the executives was concerned with the wellbeing of the company as a whole. After teambuilding relationships changed, problems were 'owned' and a vigorous programme of organization development took place. The company returned to profitability.

All teams have the same needs. Without support, little gets done. Healthy organizations are constructed of supportive teams, in which everyone feels at home

Is unsupportive teamwork a blockage in your organization?

The following activities from the companion volume, *50 Activities for Unblocking Organizational Communication*, are especially relevant:

29 Support it.
30 The Yi calendar.
31 Team roles audit.
32 Wake and mourning.
33 Eggs can leap.
34 Learnlab.
35 Product evaluation.
36 Team critique survey.

References

Belbin, M., *Management Teams – Why They Succeed and Fail*, Heinemann, 1982.
Boyatzis, R. E., *The Competent Manager*, John Wiley & Sons, 1982.
Margerison, C., *The Margerison McCann Team Management Index*, MCB Publications, 1985.

Making intelligent decisions

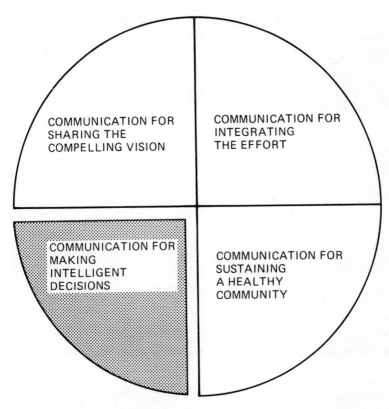

'Efficiently collecting, structuring and transmitting relevant information to those with power.'

Definitions

Intelligent – 'a superior understanding, quickness of mental apprehension, sagacity'

Decision – 'the action of deciding; settlement, determination'

Shorter Oxford Dictionary

Upward flow

Being responsive: encouraging data to flow upwards so that management knows what is going on.

Early in 1986, the space shuttle Challenger exploded thirteen seconds after launch and a presidential enquiry was established to discover the causes of the accident. It emerged that two engineers, Allan McDonald and Roger Boisjoly from Morton Thiokol, the company that built the solid fuel rockets, originally opposed the launch because they feared that the abnormally cold weather might prevent ring seals from functioning correctly. Their doubts were well-founded and probably pinpoint the problems which led to the loss of the space shuttle. Interestingly, neither engineer appears to have been rewarded for his caution. Both were stripped of their authority and staffs after the accident. The presidential enquiry concluded that there was rivalry between each of the NASA research centres. All had become secretive, but the Goddard Space Flight Centre in Huntsville, Alabama, was considered to be the worst. It was said that policy decisions were taken without reference to experts in other departments. Top executives in NASA were not told the whole truth about the risks to Challenger.

NASA failed to heed cautionary advice about Challenger's readiness to fly for two reasons. First, NASA's communication system tended to filter out dissenting views. Secondly, there were political pressures which encouraged the decision makers to say 'yes' to the launch.

Clearly there was a breakdown in upward communication. Once again we were reminded that organizations cannot operate intelligently if those with power are cut off from those with knowledge.

Intelligence is 'quickness of understanding, sagacity' (*Concise Oxford Dictionary*). Intelligent behaviour gives a capability to adjust to new circumstances and make the most of opportunities. We are accustomed to thinking of intelligence as being an individual attribute, but organizations, like individuals, need to be intelligent: that is, have quickness of understanding and sagacity.

The upward flow of communication is vital for intelligent decision making. Imagine a human brain which, after an accident, received no input from the senses and you have a vivid image of the vital importance of a constant flow of information. The management cadre, who are the 'brain of the firm', need to be open to data from below for five reasons:

o to gather information about strengths, weaknesses, opportunities and threats which confront the organization
o to harvest ideas and creativity from everyone in the organization
o to take the temperature of attitudes so that effective policies can be introduced
o to be open to challenge, thereby reducing the risk of complacency
o to be seen to be responsive, thereby satisfying people's need to feel fairly governed.

Each of these will be examined separately.

Gathering information

In one infamous First World War battle, the generals commanding British troops established themselves in comfortable quarters many miles from the front line. They moved symbols on maps, speculating about military manoeuvres. Meanwhile in the awful mud of the battlefield, thousands of young men died in fruitless attempts to vanquish a well-defended enemy. Many were drowned in water-filled shell holes. The tragedy was that the British generals did not collect information from their junior officers about the threat to their troops and believed that the battle was conducted in dry conditions. They failed to realize that the carnage was taking place in a swamp.

An earlier chapter examined the importance of communicating with the external environment. For the same reasons managers should keep in touch with the internal environment. Those with power need to gather information from within so that their decisions are firmly based. They need to assess strengths, weaknesses, opportunities and threats.

Strengths are sources of capability. They enable things to get done. Strengths include buildings, equipment, creativity systems, know-how, people, management, wealth, goodwill, image and track record. Managers need to be aware of the actual and potential strengths of their organization so that they can exploit what they control.

Weaknesses prevent strengths from being exploited. Not all missing strengths are weaknesses. A ladies' fashion shop will not have a mechanic to repair the boss's Porsche, but this is not a weakness as the task can be undertaken by the local garage. Weaknesses are the absence of *needed* strengths.

Opportunities are those possibilities which broaden, extend or deepen the quality or quantity of output of the organization. For example, a commercial company is given an opportunity by the removal of barriers in a previously closed market. Opportunities increase the possibility that an organization will survive, grow or adapt.

Threats are internal or external actions or inactions which could disadvantage the organization. A new traffic scheme may threaten a shopkeeper and the entry of a new international competitor is a threat to a large business. Threats may be political, social, economic, demographical, climatic, technological or physical.

Strengths, weaknesses, opportunities or threats need to be evaluated constantly throughout the organization. Just as a marathon runner monitors his metabolism to keep optimal performance over the full distance, so managers need valid information, which has to be gathered and transmitted upwards without oversimplifying or perverting the integrity of the data. This is done by clear success measures, sensitive routine systems, disciplined reporting structures, intensive special studies and extensive contact across hierarchical divides.

Harvesting ideas

The capacity to be intelligent is spread widely throughout organizations. In a company with five hundred employees there are as many minds capable of thinking and creativity. Equipment, libraries, history, systems and external resources add to the collective intellect of the enterprise. Upward communications systems can be seen as channels from the storehouse of corporate wisdom to those who have the power to make things happen.

For many years it has been assumed that intelligence primarily resided at the top of organizations. Those on the shopfloor were considered to be mere menials, incapable of independent thought. Managers perceived their roles as indoctrinating, instructing, and controlling, but not listening. Techniques of work study, developed as an applied science by Frederick William Taylor, exaggerated this tendency so that thinking became a function of specialists in the organization's 'technostructure'. Motivation deteriorated as people reacted with dull anger to the implied insult. The lack of interest shown by work people in the western world had few real economic consequences until growing competition from the Far East threatened their livelihood. Job enrichment, strongly advocated by Frederick Herzberg, was one of the first attempts to use the intelligence of the doers and give initiative back to ordinary people. We have seen many similar initiatives in the past twenty years.

Managers have become more aware of the need to harness human capability. For example, in 1979 an American, Gifford Pinchot III, coined the term 'intrapreneurship' as a means of encouraging enterprise within companies. Bright, vigorous and determined people are enabled to become 'intrapreneurs' and exploit their ideas to the advantage of the company. This means breaking down corporate barriers which inhibit individual creativity. The principle is to take idea-generation out of the hands of the élite.

The need for intrapreneurship has emerged from revolutions in information technology which mean that companies must now anticipate change. Simply reacting is no longer a viable strategy for survival. An excellent example of intrapreneuring is found in the American company 3M. Art Fry worked within the company and decided that self-adhesive notes were necessary and feasible. He used his political skills, enthusiasm and technical resources to develop the 'Post-it' concept. These little yellow stickers are now widespread. The traditional corporate structure is based on the assumption that the board knows best and that operating units should merely perform within defined guidelines. Many such structures are no longer viable and must be changed to stimulate greater creativity, opportunism and rapid response. In effect, creativity has to be decentralized. There is simply not enough intelligence in a small top team to do all the thinking required by today's enterprises.

The successful intrapreneur needs support, and an organizational 'godfather' provides the protection to allow ideas to germinate and grow. In effect, the intrapreneur becomes a champion, a person who fights for a cause.

This discussion has been illustrated by examples at the management level. Most people's concerns are much more mundane. I once spent some hours talking to the staff at a hospital. The administrator spoke of standards of care, cost-benefit analysis of machines and market segments. None of this, of course, had any direct relevance to the patients lying in the beds below. Fortunately the hospital administrator was a farsighted manager who had instituted a system of 'quality circles' for nursing and service staff. Weekly, under the guidance of the supervisor, all the work groups got together to discuss how things could be improved. One nurse said that the picture in room 321 was badly hung and offended a patient born in the astrological house of Libra. A secretary mentioned that an important message left on the desk had been blown on to the floor when the elevator doors were opened. A service man asked: 'Could non-slip polish be used on the floor of the pantry?' Hundreds of ideas like this were generated. Quality circles proved to be an important vehicle for upward communication.

The mechanisms for harvesting ideas are not complex. Suggestion schemes, brainstorming, quality circles, project teams and planned experiments are typical methods. All of them will work well if managers take them seriously. There are no easy answers. Commitment is essential. As people believe that their input is valued, they begin to participate. A readiness to contribute has to be channelled, and never disparaged.

Taking the temperature

The top executives of a large international corporation boasted of its reputation for enlightened industrial relations. They gave self-satisfied speeches at prestigious conferences. Then, one day, the inconceivable happened. A totally unexpected strike occurred and militant workers' representatives spoke to the press of 'years of deceit and disinterest from management'. The bitter struggle dragged on for months. One observer said: 'Negotiations are as friendly as the Pope and the Devil trying to agree who should be in charge of the Vatican on Sundays'.

What had gone wrong? Before the strike, this company's executives were infatuated with their image and failed to test the validity of their paternalistic assumptions. They did not measure the thoughts and feelings of employees, and were shocked to discover that things were much worse than they had dreamed.

There are three ways for top management to take the temperature of an organization:

o   by channelling data up through the management hierarchy
o   by direct contact between senior managers and people on the shopfloor
o   by surveys using the techniques of social science.

Communication upwards through the line is the significant source of data in most organizations, yet it is bound to be an imperfect mechanism, as demonstrated by the NASA case described at the beginning of this chapter. Top managers tend to put great weight on numerical measures which are easier for them to evaluate. Soft data, like assessments of 'esprit de corps', motivation, frustration and the like, is difficult to measure and tends to be dismissed. The most important blockages to upward communication are individuals who hold key positions of power. As one manager who worked hard to keep open said: 'I watch how people perform, listen to conversations in bars and try to get a steer on each key individual. Results are the thing, and I am very cautious of excuses. When blockages are identified they must be confronted. Ruthless implementation is necessary.' Top managers are wise to determine exactly what they want to know and ensure that subordinate managers are trained to provide this information.

Direct contact between top managers and employees is indispensable. Much that needs to be communicated is so subtle that a report writer as skilled as Charles Dickens would be needed to put reality into words. Managers have to get out of their own environments to communicate personally with people at all levels. Hewlett Packard have a management philosophy which they call 'management by walking around', which elegantly captures the message. Interestingly, cranks and misfits often give especially useful insights. Despite years of propaganda from management pundits it is commonplace to meet people who have never talked to a senior manager. One solution is to measure top managers on the extent of first-hand knowledge of employees.

Surveys using the techniques of social science can be valuable. When professionally conducted such research is systematic, impartial, meaningful and widely acceptable. Naturally there are difficulties. Sometimes it is unbelievably complex to decide what to measure, and the available tools are imprecise. Good research is costly and unwarranted expectations can be generated. In spite of these reservations, surveys are to be encouraged.

Most surveys try to measure attitudes. There are many examples of companies who have undertaken such surveys and made good use of the results. IBM, Wang, Texas Instruments and ICI are just a few of the companies committed to this way of facilitating the upward flow of communication. The survey is a technique that can easily become discredited. Management needs to listen to the findings, probe to see what they mean and institute remedial programmes. Unless this is done, a survey is considered as a palliative or an ineffectual joke.

The value of taking the temperature was well illustrated by a British company making scientific instruments. The top team had undergone a lengthy study of their role and emerged with a well devised corporate strategy. They pursued their vision of the future with great energy and agreed to a survey to collect perceptions of the workforce, expecting that little new would be revealed. Imagine the top team's alarm when they discovered that their optimistic plans were neither understood nor appreciated by the staff. In fact, the chief executive concluded: 'We need to keep on checking that we are in touch. Otherwise disaster will strike.'

Being open to challenge

The Stanhope Trust Inc. is a well-established insurance company with a developed range of products. Over many years the corporate name had become a byword for reliability. Senior executives enjoyed a most comfortable lifestyle. They were driven in Mercedes and did their work in luxurious leather-bound offices. Cocktails before lunch and golf in the afternoons typified the office day.

Meanwhile, junior managers at Stanhope began to get anxious. They looked at the ouside environment and saw upstart young insurance companies stealing business with innovative insurance policies and high-pressure selling. But the top managers of Stanhope cut themselves off from criticism and followed their traditional business approach. The cocktails came just as before, the Mercedes gleamed just as brightly.

One day, disaster struck. The Stanhope Trust announced a huge underwriting loss and its shares plunged on the stock exchange. The chief executive tried to rationalize the problem, but he and the executive committee were swept into premature retirement. A new cadre of top managers took over to implement the ideas which more junior managers had been advocating for years.

Where did the fault lie? The top management group of Stanhope had cut themselves off from challenge and complacently continued their out-of-date ways of decision making. Each top manager looked to his immediate colleagues for approval and, since this was forthcoming, they felt that proper consultation had taken place. In fact, no real challenge had occurred.

It has long been realized that power tends to corrupt. In my experience the most common corruption is a subconcious presumption of superiority. Those with authority come to believe that they are wiser, shrewder and cleverer than anyone else. Such beliefs encourage boldness but discourage dialogue. After all, if someone feels that they know best, why should they bother to listen?

In one study, the top executives in a company believed that 80 per cent of people understood the mission of the company. The opposite was the case; only 20 per cent of employees actually knew what the corporate mission was. Organizations have a particular characteristic. Things rarely happen as they are predicted. The plans which look great on paper are much more untidy in reality. Individuals behave in unusual, unpredictable, ineffective or even weird ways. Managers need to be challenged by confronting reality.

Some of the most valuable challenges into organizations come from outside the organization. The vice-president of personnel in a small company in California realized that things were bad. She found that her colleagues denied the facts. Her response was to invite a business school professor to give a day's training on 'cause of corporate collapse'. The effect was electrifying. For the first time, senior managers realized the importance of warning signs and had a way to conceptualize their malaise. The challenge from outside had a catalytic effect.

There is no substitute for challenge. Perfect systems cannot be created. Those who hold power need to answer difficult questions. Only critical interplay between people with sharp minds enables assumptions to be tested and sloppy thinking exposed. The ancient Greeks were right when they considered skilful argument to be among the highest of skills.

Being seen to respond

As political democracies replaced feudal or despotic states, people became accustomed to having the right to be heard. Democratic governments are open to influence. People expect élites to understand their views, even though the final decision may go against them.

Organizations mirror the political context. Managers need to be seen to be open. Wise managers have learned the importance of listening, and being seen to listen. This is the clearest way of demonstrating that power is being exercised with care and consideration. Note: it is not enough to be absorbed in what is said, you have to be prepared to listen.

The management style which best captures this principle is the 'open door approach'. Many managers claim that their door is always open for observations, concerns, ideas and complaints. Of course there are two doors – one physical and the other psychological. The open door approach only works when both doors are ajar.

Managers have a difficult task. Those who are perceived to be easily influenced are deemed weak and insubstantial. At the other end of the scale, those who are impervious to influence are seen to be ignorant, domineering or isolated. Even managers who choose an authoritarian approach gain from being perceived as responsive. One chief executive put it this way: 'I know that I have to win support. This means that people have to give me the benefit of the doubt. Often they don't understand the issues involved. My tactic is to ensure that I'm seen. I make myself accessible. I listen and show that I understand. This way they know that I care.'

Upward communication is especially important in organizations which exist to serve personal needs. For example, the borough council in Richmond issued the following statement to ratepayers: 'We want to know your views … The council has held dozens of public consultation meetings, and you have sent us thousands of tear-off slips with your views … We ask your views and then do what you ask. We promised to make the council less remote and to involve people more in the running of the council. We now have mobile offices at eight different locations every week to make the council easier to 'get at' … No major decisions are taken now without public consultation beforehand.'

This chapter started with a description of the loss of the space shuttle Challenger. There have been many cases where decisions have been taken in spite of strong evidence that the choice was wrong. The quality of decision making is dependent on the breadth and depth of intelligence available. Organizations centralize power to provide incisive direction, but by doing this they can reduce the majority to playing the role of cyphers and drones. This may have been desirable in the past, but today's organizations need all the brainpower they can get.

Is defective upward flow a blockage in your organization?

The following activities from the companion volume, *50 Activities for Unblocking Organizational Communication*, are especially relevant:

37 Communication transactions.
38 Group feedback.
39 Brainstorming.

Apt administration

Being efficient: not having excessively cumbersome and costly channels for communication.

The top executives of a nationwide chain of retail stores began to worry about the sheer quantity of paperwork that was clogging up the company. Forms proliferated, endless reports were prepared, and copious statistical analyses fluttered through the organization like fallen leaves on a windy winter's day. Executives added up the cost of all this communication and their calculations looked as if they were computing the distance to the nearest star. Vast amounts of money were being consumed to keep an inefficient administrative machine ticking over.

What could be done to rid the company of the scourge of excessive communication? Shock tactics were decided upon. Every piece of paper used during the course of one day was collected, and the resulting mound placed in the entrance hall of the corporate head office. Employees had to walk around a huge heap of paperwork on their way to work.

This obstacle course symbolized the need for change. The company initiated a vigorous campaign to reduce paperwork. Every form was analysed to see whether it could be simplified or eliminated. New systems were devised and circulation lists, which had grown like unattended brambles, were pruned back. Everyone was told to find more economical ways of communication.

It worked. Unnecessary paperwork was largely eliminated and the administrative machine began to provide useful data for decision making. A successful campaign was fought against excessive bureaucracy which had multiplied through lack of thought, unsystematic thinking and neglect. Management sought to devise an administration system that was apt – defined as 'suitable, prompt and quick-witted'.

This meant eliminating 'red tape'. The term in most people's minds, is associated with the labyrinthine processes of government bureaucracy, but it is found in many other organizations. Red tape means 'excessive formality or attention to routine. Rigid or mechanical adherence to rules and regulations.' It is expensive, tortuous and energy-consuming. Organizations with red tape suffer from stultified decision making.

Administrative systems often proliferate and become etched like deep river valleys in the landscape of the organization. Systems that cross departmental boundaries are hardest to change. Organizations inadvertently become victims of a formality that was conceived in good faith but has grown grotesque through time.

One of the most frequent complaints about communication is 'There is too much of it: paperwork, statistics, reports, reading...'. Managers argue that their time is wasted by continuous demands to supply information. Opportunities are lost as managers become data providers rather than creative thinkers.

The cost of routine communication is rarely evaluated. A report may require many hours of work and expensive computer time, yet scant attention is often paid to such documents. They are consigned to the waste paper basket without a second glance. The cost of red tape can be enormous.

The Communist world enjoyed little economic growth in the early 1980s. Why? Mikhail Gorbachev blamed turgid organizations and over-bureaucratic procedures. For example, Soviet economist, Alexei Rumyantsey, writing in *Trud* magazine, estimated in 1983 that the Soviet bureaucracy was generating over 800 billion documents per year. The concern with petty bureaucracy was found at all levels of the system – amongst other things, the Soviet Union's supreme decision-making body had considered whether to lower the price of fur collars on winter overcoats.

Red tape grows fastest when power is over-centralized, trust is low, and those in authority are defensive. Organizations become unresponsive and inhumane when formality replaces intelligence and routine is pursued for its own sake. Much organizational communication is continued for reasons of history and tradition. Procedures are devised as new requirements surface and, before long, massive resources are spent in maintaining communication systems which no one controls. Only when something extraordinary happens, like the purchase of a new computer, is a systematic study undertaken.

It is tempting to write a homily that says little more than 'excessive bureaucracy, formality and paperwork is bad, so cut it out'. This would be worse than useless. We would have identified a problem but provided little insight into its cause.

Babies can be washed out with the bath water! Not all systems and procedures are an unmitigated evil. Organizations must formally co-ordinate and regulate their myriad activities. Imagine that you had to run an airport, issue a million driving licences or collect a weekly payment from ten thousand households – such tasks need 'suitable, prompt and quick-witted administrative systems'.

Administration brings order and predictability. An underdeveloped organization is crippled by inadequate systems. As one manager in an out-of-control business observed: 'It's a farce here. The Marx brothers couldn't have imagined the script. If we've got it we'll lose it. There's no control, no co-ordination and no discipline.'

Organizations must be efficient information systems. Decision makers need accurate information quickly, without becoming lost in a mess of unwanted data. They want the right data in the right place at the right time.

The need is obvious but it is immensely difficult to meet these requirements in practice. A chief administrator of an international charity illustrated the point when she complained: 'All the hard data I get is historical. It tells me where we've been and not where we are going. This is especially true of finance specialists. At best they only give a snapshot of the present. All our systems are set up to identify problems, not ensure good performance. I badly need better information.'

How elaborate should administrative systems be? The answer is that they should mirror the complexity of the organization. Consider a small company which farms and sells watercress. The task is relatively simple and administration can be rudimentary. Conversely, a complex organization needs elaborate systems. The American Pentagon must keep alert to military situations everywhere in the world and therefore needs information systems of mind-boggling complexity.

An organization must incorporate the variety of its environment in its systems. Underdeveloped administration deprives management of essential information so that they cannot respond to the diversity and subtlety of the environment. If this happens, the organization, like a long-term incumbent in an institution, loses touch with reality and cannot take intelligent decisions.

The story becomes more involved. With increasing complexity in the environment we find that different groups and departments specialize more. In effect, it becomes harder for the left hand to understand what the right hand is doing. Formal communication systems must ensure that the organization does not degenerate into self-administered and warring factions. This is done by establishing multidisciplinary project teams, appointing specialist co-ordinators, carefully balancing power between groups and rewarding departmental co-operation.

Only the initiative of top management can establish a suitable, prompt and quick-witted administrative framework. It is unrealistic to expect departmental managers to identify and resolve broad needs. A managerial overview is needed to ensure that appropriate systems are developed. Of course, the analytical leg work may be done by project teams, communication specialists or consultants.

In order to understand why inadequate or inappropriate administrative systems undermine organizational intelligence, we have to return to the ideas in the chapter on 'Integrating mechanisms'. You may recall that five types of organization were described, using Henry Mintzberg's model.

The remainder of this chapter builds on that earlier discussion, so it is important that you have Henry's model clearly in your mind. Here is a brief reminder of the five organizational types.

1 Simple structure

Everyone works for one boss who makes all the key decisions and knows what is going on. There is little formality and much opportunism.

2 Machine bureaucracy

An organization with elaborate specification of roles, hierarchies, job descriptions and careful control over processes.

3 Professional bureaucracy

Highly qualified individuals are enabled to perform their specialized services for clients by this organization. Professionals have power to decide how things should be done.

4 Divisionalized form

Larger organizations are often broken into product/market units or divisions. These are given a good deal of autonomy and develop as semi-independent businesses.

5 Adhocracy

This is an organization which makes use of flexible and rapidly developing combinations of experts who make temporary (ad hoc) arrangements to get novel things done. Such organizations are creative and fast moving.

Is it all coming back to you? If these ideas are still hazy, it would be useful to review the five types of organization in more depth (see pages 64–70).

What have organizational types got to do with devising suitable, prompt and quick-witted administration? Imagine you were about to fly from New York to Tokyo and discovered that the aircraft engineers had no written procedures for checking whether maintenance work had been done. Would you board the aeroplane happily? Or imagine a patient on the operating table. Each time the surgeon wants to use a knife or a stitch, a form must be sent to the administration block for authorization. Endless haggling between administrators and surgeons is commonplace. Would you let this hospital take out your appendix?

The first example – the flight engineering team – needs a high degree of predictability and reliability. The experts at Boeing or British Aerospace have studied the precise tightness for each bolt and the aircraft maintenance organization is designed to ensure that the rules are applied. But in the second illustration it must be the surgeon who decides in an instant what needs to be done. Power must be in the hands of the expert holding the knife.

Getting administration right, therefore, is a more complex concept than it first appears. Returning to the five organizational types, we can take the analysis further.

In the 'simple structure' excessive formality is rarely seen. I remember establishing my first small business some years ago. When the time came to submit the annual accounts the unsorted receipts were in shoeboxes, and it was only with the tolerant help of a systematic friend that the accounts could be prepared. Red tape was totally absent! Even rudimentary systems were lacking; the embryonic business actually needed formality and bureaucracy. Later, a new employee joined the team and she insisted on strict procedures which were welcomed as saviours.

This example is typical. Most simple structures are not elaborate because the founder could operate with minimal administrative machinery. Should the enterprise grow, or the founder move on, then successors are much less likely to be able to manage from the seats of their pants.

Occasionally the boss of a simple structure is a brilliant administrator. Sherlock Holmes spent many hours compiling records which we would now call his data base. After one case he asked Watson: 'Just give me down my index of biographies from the shelf,' and then went on to turn 'the pages lazily, leaning back in his chair and blowing great clouds of smoke from his cigar. "My collection of M's is a fine one," said he. "Moriarty himself is enough to make any letter illustrious, and here is Morgan the poisoner, and Merridew of abominable memory, and Matthews, who knocked out my left canine in the waiting room at Charing Cross, and, finally, here is our friend of tonight".' (*The Return of Sherlock Holmes*, p. 26). We can learn from Sherlock Holmes who ran a simple structure but compiled extensive, accessible and meaningful records. Today he would probably carry a portable microcomputer and keep records of lurid crimes and evil criminals on mini-floppy disks.

Despite the rare competence of Sherlock Holmes, formal communication in simple structures tends to be underdeveloped. It is likely that information is neither collected nor processed efficiently. The boss often fails to use systematic administrative systems or up-to-date technology. Progress, sometimes survival, requires formality and discipline.

In the 'machine bureaucracy' there is a very different situation. Here everything is documented. I am a consultant to an international electronics company that has a manual of procedures which includes telling staff what kinds of wine to buy for customers' lunches, and specifies the exact typeface to be used on overhead projector slides.

Control is exercised through specification of processes and so the technical quality of controls is paramount. The Jaguar story, in the first chapter, provides a useful illustration. You will recall that the new chief executive, John Egan, had a virtually bankrupt company when he took over in 1980. He used a scythe to cut out excess resources. Interestingly, not everywhere was cut; Egan hired more people in the engineering function. He argued that high quality engineering surveillance was essential to ensure well-put-together cars. Jaguar needed better standardization.

In poorly managed machine bureacracies, red tape stimulates growth in informal communication or 'grapevines'. Unresponsive and unwieldy systems are circumvented by backdoor arrangements. People get their information through personal contacts. There is fertile ground for politics and nepotism to thrive. The informal system, however, is not always counterproductive. Ironically, some of the most valuable initiatives are taken outside official channels.

Ill-conceived or poorly managed administration dampens enthusiasm and strangles initiative. People become part of a system, functioning in a cosy world of forms, procedures, reports and protocols. Nothing is urgent or special. So there is no possibility of exploiting the creative power of anxiety and the value of desperation. At first sight, emotion may seem counterproductive, but consider the situation of a chief executive who finds his products nearing the end of their life-cycle and has no ready substitutes. Top management is pressurizing by asking questions. Perhaps the shareholders or banks begin to withdraw support. The workforce is showing anxieties. Trade union representatives detect potential problems and blame the management. Scare stories in the local newspaper may add to the pressure. Alarm, insecurity, anxiety and naked fear are present. Emotions communicate more than the words. Urgency, by itself, can be blind and lead to panic. But, when structured, it excites enthusiasm, releases initiative and cuts through red tape.

There is a way to attack convoluted, wasteful and inadequate administration systems. The computer has proved especially potent. Computers increase opportunities to control behaviour. In machine bureaucracies many of the measures are quantifiable and predictable, so computerized systems are well able to cope. There are many illustrations. Until recently, postmen sorted letters by hand whereas now computers can handle this task. Stock control in most retail chains is done by computer. Airline tickets are written by printers attached to a worldwide network.

The computer has proved to be an effective weapon. Overblown and labyrinthine systems must be simplified before computers are installed. The result of computerization is generally a fundamental evaluation of information systems. Computerized communication systems provide a capacity to control complex machine-like systems relatively cheaply, thereby increasing their manageability. As one manager in a motor manufacturing plant said: 'We have never operated with this level of controllability before'. This has profound implications for machine bureaucracies as intelligent computer systems now permit substantial increases in flexibility and capability.

Technology amplifies the capabilities of managers for good or ill. An error is magnified many times by effective technology. Faster administration means less time to correct mistakes. Fewer numbers of management personnel decrease the checks and balances in the management cadre. For these reasons it is even more important to manage information technology so as to avoid cumbersome or unresponsive communication and decision-making systems.

The 'professional bureaucracy' is different again. In schools, universities, agencies and hospitals it is difficult to find out what is really going on. This chapter was revised while I was in hospital for a few days. Watching the hospital at work gave a vivid illustration. Each doctor had a batch of patients, loosely organized by the type of ailment they suffered from. However, one patient had three malaises – earache, a kidney disorder and a skin rash. Despite strenuous efforts by the senior nursing officer, it proved impossible to get the ENT surgeon, kidney specialist and dermatologist together to provide an integrated programme of care for the unfortunate patient. Power is decentralized in professional bureaucracies.

The difficulty that the patient with three ailments experienced was that power was in the hands of professionals who specialized in treating only one part of the body. The ear, nose and throat surgeon was as uninterested in the patient's skin as a florist would be in the contents of a fishmonger's shop. Because patients have both ears and skin the medical distinctions cannot really remain separate. Effective administration should integrate the work of specialists. This is difficult to orchestrate while each specialist concentrates on a narrow expertise.

The role of management in devising apt administration in such organizations merits further discussion. Managers are either senior professionals or administrators qualified in management sciences. Both have difficulties. Senior professionals are likely to be wedded to their own disciplines, intolerant of administration and cavalier in their attitudes to spending money. Career administrators are likely to be derided as insensitive bureaucrats, obsessed with financial control and politically outmanoeuvred by long-established professionals. Long chains of procedures are devised to authorize requests. Especially when money is tight the budget becomes the focus of discontent and, in an effort to control costs, managers put more effort into surveillance – much to the annoyance of professionals who want to expand their own expertise.

Individual professionals must be allowed to exercise their skills within an overall vision of the future which integrates the work of everyone in the professional bureaucracy. Inevitably, power is shared. The essence of high-performing professional bureaucracies is sustaining balance between the needs of the organization and the professionals who make it work.

The fourth type of organization, the 'divisionalized form' was devised as an elegant administrative solution to the potential problem of over-centralized decision taking. Most of the illustrations are from the world of commerce but, for variety, consider a military case study – when at its height the Roman Empire had such countries as England, Egypt and much of what is now the Soviet Union within its 6,000 mile border. In the second century, Rome was able to control some 50 million people with an army of just 300,000 well equipped and superbly trained soldiers. Their military strategy was based on key fortresses along the frontiers. As the border was threatened local commanders had all the resources to deal with the situation themselves. Later, in the third century, the policy was reversed and the centre became the heart of military might. The abandonment of the divisionalized structure was one of the factors that led to the downfall of the Roman Empire in 476 AD.

The jargon of today tells us that the Roman Empire operated as a divisionalized form during its most successful years. Strong local commanders took total responsibility for their regions and Rome exercised overall strategic control. There was a clear separation of duties between the Emperor and the fortress commandants. Apt administration was encouraged by well-defined limits of authority.

However, central leaderships faltered as emperors pursued their licentious and drunken debauches rather than settling down to strategic planning conferences. The empire began to fall apart. Power was taken from the divisional commanders and given to crazed and ignorant hedonistic sots. Nero fiddled while Rome burned. The integrity of the organizational concept was destroyed and Rome declined and fell.

In the divisionalized form of organization it is vital that accurate information on performance is rapidly processed upwards. Strategic decisions require an enormous amount of data. These have to be collected and sifted, summarized and put into sensible formats. Such 'filters' need regular attention to ensure that they do their job properly. This is especially difficult to manage in decentralized organizations. For example, it was shown that the filtering procedures did not work well in the British Government's decision-making system immediately before the Falkland Islands crisis in 1982. Crucial information was not passed to a Cabinet committee which, therefore, could not make an informed assessment of risk.

Despite the difficulties of strategic decision taking, when there is a developed command, control and intelligence system, the divisionalized form is essential to managing organizations today. It permits a focus on a particular product or market and can provide a nice balance between centralized control and autonomy.

The last form of organization is the 'adhocracy'. This buzzing and creative mêlée of frequently changing structures is best illustrated by an example. I was asked to work as a consultant to an ad hoc team whose task was to design a common chassis for a wide range of electric and gas cookers. All the relevant experts were assembled, bright engineers, designers, production experts, planners and marketing specialists.

At the start there was no organization or role description. Everything had to be done from scratch. The team members had to get to know each other, set up a temporary organization, clarify objectives, agree a process of work and keep changing their organization over the busy weeks in which the new chassis design was devised. The creativity was infectious. One participant remarked: 'I know the goal but who the hell knows what's going to happen next? The synergy is fantastic. Meetings are constantly being called, and each one changes something important. The process is unpredictable. Really exciting.'

Adhocracies are destroyed by rigid administrative frameworks. Systems, procedures, conventions and protocols all undermine the vigour of the adhocracy. People with expertise working informally together is the only way to make an adhocracy work.

The search for apt administration

Each of these five organizational types needs different disciplines of formal communication. The simple structure is often excessively dependent on one person and lacks useful systems. The machine bureaucracy must be tightly controlled but can become strangled by inappropriate regulation. Professional bureaucracies become excessively fragmented as power is captured by isolated individuals. The divisionalized form is measured on short-term performance and so becomes excessively preoccupied with immediate events to the detriment of long-term health. Adhocracies are hotbeds of innovation, but notoriously difficult to control; they depend on excellent informal communication.

Each form of organization must conduct a search for an administrative system that is suitable, prompt and quick-witted, but the nature of the enemy varies in each case.

○ in the simple structure it is a war against undeveloped or immature systems
○ in the machine bureaucracy it is a war against unintelligent systems
○ in the professional bureaucracy it is a war against fragmented and repressive systems
○ in the divisionalized form it is a war against short-term financial systems and head office interference
○ in the adhocracy it is a war against rigid systems.

In order to be 'apt' administrative systems must:

○ enable the organization to work well
○ reduce the inherent weaknesses in the chosen form of organization
○ to be as elaborate and diverse as the environment which the organization seeks to control.

All organizations need intelligent and helpful administration. One interesting example is drawn from a police force in Northern England with a total staff of 5,154. They recognized that officers were spending valuable time on unnecessary paperwork and that some duplication of effort was taking place. The Police Organization Studies Department set up 'Project paperchase', an eighteen-month experiment to reduce the time spent by officers on clerical work. The solutions included new systems and investment in helpful technology. Taken together, all the improvements led to a 30 per cent reduction in the time spent by police officers on routine clerical duties.

A note of caution! The effort to simplify administrative systems can be overdone. A party of students were taken to visit a company which had just completed a scourge of its paperwork systems. They spoke to a manager who demonstrated how the new philosophy worked. He took a memo from his in-tray, made a brief note in his diary, then ostentatiously tore the memorandum into pieces and tossed them into the waste paper basket. The students were impressed and went on to the next office. However, one student had forgotten her glasses and returned to collect them. She found the manager guiltily sticking the torn memorandum together. It emerged that he kept a private filing system in his garage at home, just in case.

Administration is a much maligned characteristic of organizations. It has become a buzzword which allows the ignorant observer to believe that there are simple solutions to complex organizational ills. This chapter has argued that the quality of decision making is dependent on devising apt administrative processes which are neither immature nor over-elaborate.

Is inapt administration a blockage in your organization?

The following activities from the companion volume, *50 Activities for Unblocking Organizational Communication*, are especially relevant:

41 Improving intergroup communication.
43 Band Aid.

Communication skills

Being effective: people have the ability to communicate well.

Ronald Reagan was not a noted intellectual, but as President of the USA he had to take decisions of great complexity. Experts on foreign affairs, defence, law and economics lined up for his attention. Each expert wanted the President to make a decision on highly involved and contentious matters. How was this done?

Fascinating techniques were developed. President Reagan learned well from television, and videos were made to brief him for the fireside summit with Mikhail Gorbachev in 1985. Teams of illustrators and cartoonists worked at the White House to bring complex issues down to earth.

Robert Stockman, once Reagan's director of the Office of Management and Budgets, reports that he devised a multiple-choice budget quiz to help the President understand the issues involved in making budget cuts. The quiz gave the President fifty choices, and his task was to review each item, decide whether to cut deeply, lightly or not at all. Apparently, the President was entranced with the quiz and spent hours, pencil in hand, deliberating on the options. Stockman was delighted; he had found a way of communicating some of the most difficult choices to a president who was uncomfortable with intellectual pursuits.

All of those who presented information to him had to be skilled individual communicators, otherwise the President was likely to become bored and go for a game of golf.

The skills of the communicator make a real difference to the intelligence of individuals, governments and organizations. This does not only apply to management. Every day, in any sizeable organization, there are millions of communication transactions. You can imagine what is happening by visualizing electrical activity in the brain. It is impossible to analyse each act of information exchange but it is crucial that this buzz of communication enables intelligent decisions to be made.

Effective communication skills are especially important in today's organizations. Routine jobs are becoming increasingly mechanized, automated or computerized. More people are dealing with non-routine situations, unexpected problems and strategic decision making. Such tasks require a high order of personal communication skills. The pressure is on. People must work together skilfully to solve complex problems.

What are personal communication skills? The following extract from a description of a candidate for a management job gives some vital clues.

Elvis Woodman is widely recognized as an effective manager. He took initiatives to learn about good interpersonal relationships by attending training workshops. He has thought deeply about how his personality affects others. He is sensitive without being soft. He is attentive to what others say and do. He is an excellent listener who quickly gains rapport with people. As a leader he is capable of giving support or direction as appropriate. In meetings he uses a logical approach to solving problems and seizing opportunities. When difficulties occur he acknowledges the emotional aspects but delves into the facts so as to make a positive decision. In groups, he is capable of steering other people constructively and dealing with destructive people. Those who work with him develop new insights and skills. He encourages others to make the most of their potential. He stimulates new ideas and is open to positive criticism.

This is a description of a skilled communicator. By studying the details on Elvis Woodman we can analyse twelve primary ingredients of effective personal communication skills. Most of them are also relevant to other white-collar workers.

○ accurate perception of how one's personality affects others
    (self-insight)
○ prepared to stand firm (assertion)

○ good listening skills (active listening)
○ supportive and directive leadership as necessary (leadership)
○ methodical approach to problem solving and decision making (systematic approach)
○ acknowledges the importance of feeling and emotion (counselling)
○ capable of steering meetings well (chairmanship)
○ able to deal with unco-operative people (interpersonal problem solving)
○ developing the competence of others (trainer competence)
○ prepared to consider and implement new ideas (creativity)
○ able to communicate effectively through the written word (writing skills)
○ able to communicate effectively through the spoken word (oral communication competence).

These twelve communication skills are valuable to all managers. Where they are lacking, the quality of decision making in the organization suffers. In order to clarify how this happens, we will examine briefly each of the twelve skills.

1 Self-insight

Self-insight is gained as we reflect on ourselves, experience new situations and receive feedback from others. We become clearer about our own values and potential, understanding our unique character so that we can be more true to our nature. Such insight is hard to quantify or convey to others. The quest for self-understanding is always a personal search.

Self-insight is valuable to managers because:

○ an inaccurate self-concept irritates, upsets or distresses other people
○ people with high self-insight seem to be able to handle stress and pressure
○ self-insight improves objectivity.

A practical way of deepening self-insight is by gathering feedback from others. The term 'feedback' describes the process whereby a person gains information about the impression he or she makes on others. Training programmes have been devised to help develop sensitivity to others. Small groups, which develop a close and supportive climate, enable participants to be truthful about themselves and how they perceive others. An extraordinary exchange of insights takes place which can have a profound effect on all involved.

2 Assertion

It is a common observation that some people are much better at getting their own way than others. The ability to be firm, clear and personally powerful is termed 'assertiveness'.

Assertiveness is valuable to managers because:

○ energy is released and the person feels stronger
○ other people take more notice of an assertive manager
○ good ideas get the hearing they deserve
○ dominant people are less likely to get away with bullying behaviour
○ relationships with others improve – difficulties are resolved rather than festering underneath the surface.

Managers can increase their assertiveness in a practical way by attending specialized seminars which help them to examine their personal backgrounds and identify attitudes which inhibit the expression of natural assertion. Such seminars teach special assertion skills such as delivering clear messages, avoiding 'flak', repeating your point, giving emphasis etc. Assertion seminars are especially useful for minority or disadvantaged groups like black or women managers.

3 Active listening

It is difficult to listen to others. Other peoples' inputs may be regarded as an unwelcome interruption of your line of thought. Some people even say: 'I don't have time to listen!' Unless you are truly concerned to hear others' viewpoints, the motivation to listen is inadequate. You need to develop 'relaxed concentration' that signals to others 'I am ready to hear you'. There are special techniques to assist the active listener, like reflecting, summarizing, clarifying and probing.

Active listening is valuable to managers because:

○ more data are available
○ more good ideas are voiced
○ problems are aired rather than repressed
○ relationships with others are improved
○ people feel more committed to their work.

A practical way of improving listening skills is to practice and get feedback on your own capability. Active listening is a set of skills that, like riding a bicycle, can be learned and improved. Effective listeners are made, not born.

4 Leadership skills

Effective leadership is a crucial set of communication skills. Fortunes have been lost through the use of inappropriate leadership styles. Organizations apparently suffering death throes have been 'reborn' under excellent leadership. Truly outstanding leaders become folk heroes and are revered in our hearts and minds. Effective leaders have two outstanding qualities: the capacity to devise and communicate a 'compelling vision' (see chapter on this subject) and the communication skills needed to support and direct those who follow them.

'Supportive behaviour' means that you must get to know subordinates, concern yourself with what they think and feel, and encourage them to give their best. 'Directive behaviour' means telling subordinates what to do and instructing them in the right way to do it. Each follower requires a blend of support and direction depending on his or her willingness and ability to perform particular tasks. As people become more able so they require less directive behaviour from their leader; as they become more willing so they require less supportive behaviour from their leader.

Leadership skills are valuable to managers because:

○ most managers are measured on their ability to perform in this role
○ unsatisfactory behaviour is reduced
○ overall standards improve

o people give more of their natural ability so they have greater job satisfaction
o the organization benefits through improved exploitation of talents.

Managers can improve their leadership skills in practical ways with specialized training courses, imitation, on-the-job counselling and coaching. They can benefit from obtaining feedback on their existing style, often collected by questionnaires completed by subordinates. These data, when discussed, reveal strengths and weaknesses. In addition, there are many training exercises which stimulate leadership situations ranging from intellectually demanding business games to hazardous wilderness projects.

5 Systematic approach

For many years army officers studied decision making and realized that there were disciplines which, if rigorously followed, resulted in fewer blunders and a greater chance of victory. A structured approach enables decision makers to make wiser choices between considered options.

Non-military organizations have the same needs. They have been forced to cope with an increasing rate of change and have come to realize the great benefit of a structured approach to problem solving and decision making. As one manager put it: 'We found that there was a technology for finding answers to difficult questions, rather than depending on a hunch or toss of a coin'.

Systematic approaches to problem solving and decision making emphasize rational, logical, rigorous and methodical attitudes and skills. They draw from the best traditions of scientific research, but need to incorporate intuitive and creative processes.

A systematic approach is valuable to managers because:

o problems are solved effectively
o decisions are more intelligent
o managers are less likely to be overwhelmed and suffer stress
o leadership ability is improved
o meetings are more effective

○ time is saved as people devote less effort to unrewarding pursuits.

There are practical ways to improve your capacity to use a systematic approach by trial and error learning, first-hand experiences, reading, watching experts at work and participating in specialized training courses. When managers discover the value of a systematic discipline it is a small jump for them to realize the tremendous benefits in the day-by-day management job.

6 Counselling

At first sight it may seem strange that counselling is included in a list of communication skills for managers. It is often believed that management is a rough and tough occupation and has no place for the 'soft' skills of a counsellor. This is not the case. Human behaviour is influenced by feelings and emotions. Managers should be practitioners in the art of building constructive relationships. This requires the counsellor's sensitivities and skills.

Counselling helps people to understand themselves better, to resolve personal problems and to take a truthful but positive approach to life. It requires that feelings and emotions be respected, even if they appear illogical. Managers will not wish to delve into the complex topic of therapeutic counselling, but they can improve their ability to cope with feelings such as anger, frustration, stress, depression, anxiety, pride, enthusiasm and fear.

Counselling is valuable to managers because:

○ the manager relates to others more effectively
○ people with personal or work problems can be helped
○ potentially serious problems are detected earlier
○ emotional factors are taken into account when planning change, so action plans have a greater chance of success.

You can improve your counselling skills by guided practice and review. A framework of concepts is a useful starting point but skills are only developed by practice. Supportive but critical feedback is essential. In particular, closed circuit television assists managers to develop a skilful but authentic style.

7 Chairmanship

Some managers detest meetings and believe that they are the epitomy of all that is bad in organizational life. Yet meetings are constantly held, often at huge expense, for no one can think of a better mechanism for exchange of information, co-ordination, decision making or planning. Despite their drawbacks, meetings are the most ubiquitous integrating mechanism and are with us to stay.

Few individuals have the skills and wisdom to behave impeccably in meetings, so discipline and control are needed. This role is played by a chairman who acts as the 'process manager' and exploits human resources towards objectives. Chairmanship requires many of the skills described in this chapter, especially a high order of self-insight. You must clarify objectives, systematic approach, encourage or control members and build bridges between factions.

Chairmanship is valuable to managers because:

o   ineffective meetings waste time and resources
o   effective meetings are better able to make decisions and solve problems
o   effective chairmen tend to have more progressive careers
o   participants respect competent chairmanship
o   action plans are more likely to result.

You can improve your chairmanship skills by observing a 'master' at work, coaching in real situations, and attending specialized training seminars which provide a combination of theory, skill training and practice. Sound intellectual competence is a necessary qualification for the role. Equally important, the chairman should have a measured personality which is capable of integrating different personalities.

8 Interpersonal problem solving

It is comparatively easy to relate to others who behave nicely. Friendly, supportive, rational and interested people provoke few interpersonal problems. But a person who is unfriendly, unsupportive, irrational or disinterested may be rightly described as 'a pain in the tail'.

Six important questions will help you to solve a difficult relationship:

1   How is your own approach contributing to the problem?
2   What precise differences in behaviour do you want to see?
3   How does the 'difficult' person or group see the issues?
4   What kinds of power are you attempting to use and why are they not being effective?
5   Do you have a conscious strategy for influencing which escalates from feedback and counselling to firm disciplinary action?
6   What are you going to do if your strategy fails?

Interpersonal problem solving is valuable to managers because:

o   low performing people are confronted and performance may improve
o   the manager feels stronger and more potent
o   high performance is encouraged because people see that interpersonal problems are being positively tackled.

A practical way to develop your interpersonal problem-solving skills is through 'learning by experience', under the guidance of a mentor. Techniques can be taught but the most useful insights come through experiment, feedback and counselling.

9   Trainer competence

One of the key tasks of a manager is to become increasingly redundant by developing others. This approach strikes fear into the hearts of the insecure but it is the only progressive way to manage. Training and developing are essential tools for improving the quality of performance. Some managers think of training as a low priority assignment which distracts them from their primary task of getting things done. This is an unproductive stance; in fact, training is one of the most powerful managerial weapons available.

Training techniques include instructing, experimenting, counselling, coaching, getting feedback, distance learning, team building, reviewing, appraisal and project assignment. These techniques can often be used informally; there is no need for special facilities or equipment. Managers can develop their areas into 'learning environments' and thereby gain greater resourcefulness and improved motivation.

Trainer competence is valuable to managers because:

o managers have an acceptable technique for controlling behaviour
o morale is raised as people become more competent
o inadequate performance is reduced
o standards of output are improved in quality, quantity and reliability.

You can develop your training competence by reading, coaching and attending specialized training courses. Managers benefit from acquiring some of the skills of a good teacher, especially a sound awareness of the stages of human development and what factors help or hinder adult learning.

10 Creativity

Industrial and technological change has a great impact on managers today. The only constructive response to external threat is to counter attack with innovation and a rigorous questioning of the status quo. Managers must become bolder and more creative.

Communicating for creativity requires different attitudes and skills from those required to maintain an existing situation. You have to generate ideas, collect information, undertake research, evaluate risks and make choices. The creative individual works with others to look beyond the conventional and grapple with uncertainty and confusion. Decisions have to be taken with inadequate information so gifted people become skilled at making hunches. Insight seems to come from the darker recesses of the mind as the subconscious self contributes powerful but subtle information.

Generating ideas is only part of the creative process; new concepts and methods must be communicated to others. Creativity is not always easy to handle. Divergent and radical ideas are seductive. Innovation can be undertaken without sound preparation as excitement takes over from common sense. Successful creativity requires that new approaches work in the real world. Managers must learn how to manage dialogue between imagination and realism if they are to play a truly creative but practical role.

Creativity is valuable to managers because:

○ creative managers are more likely to cope effectively with problems and opportunities
○ both the quality and quantity of decision making improves as managers and teams become more creative
○ individual managers get more challenge and satisfaction from their jobs
○ the customers of the organization obtain better products or services
○ competitive advantage is more likely to be sustained.

Practical ways to develop your creativity are by self-study, practising creative techniques, team building and project work. The basis of creative achievement is freedom in oneself; so the individual has to examine personal blockages to creativity. Assignments can help by forcing the individual into situations where creativity is demanded. Creative individuals need to learn how to contribute their ideas to others constructively.

11 Writing skills

Most managers spend a lot of their time reading, writing and analysing statistics. Their task is to manage what is too complex for a computer to handle. They also have to look ahead and decide what could and should be done. Improvements to buildings, production technologies, changes in markets, revised personnel policies are just a few of the topics to be considered. Such matters are complex and arguable. A written analysis is essential to sharpen debate and give a balanced presentation of facts.

The skills of writing include word choice, sentence construction, paragraphing, logical argument, report structuring and graphical presentation. Behind such skills lie expertise in logical thinking, appropriate use of concepts, story telling and practical orientation. Discussion papers, reports and proposals are only part of the manager's written output. Visual aids for presentations, letters, memoranda, and regular reports are also required.

Writing skills are required throughout the hierarchy. A technician must be capable of writing well-considered reports and a sales clerk able to write lucid and balanced letters. These written documents present the image of the company to the outside world. The capacity to write well is especially important at senior levels. The complexity of managing a large organization requires substantial intellectual competence which can only be communicated through the written word.

Writing skills are valuable to managers because:

o   important ideas are more likely to be considered
o   complex situations can be better explored
o   more thought is devoted to considering written submissions
o   writing something down is a valuable discipline
o   people are judged on the quality of their written work.

You can develop your writing skills by accepting critique from acknowledged experts or by attending short training workshops which teach the elements of preparing written work. Managers can also learn by imitation: examine highly regarded written documents and see how they have been constructed.

12   Oral communication skills

The presentation of the spoken word used to be considered a great skill. Greek and Roman leaders were taught the art of oratory. They became highly competent in conveying important ideas and swaying emotions in speeches and conversation.

Today few of us have been trained as orators, yet the skills remain valid. As Shakespeare's Mark Antony said: 'Friends, Romans, countrymen, Lend me your ears'. Managers too are assessed on their capacity to be coherent, confident and persuasive when they present their views and ideas in speech.

Oral communication skills include accurate choice of words, logical flow, full explanation, avoidance of digression or redundant information, objectivity and capacity to hold interest. The good speaker uses every word to add impact. Care is taken to balance seriousness with humour. Visual presentation adds to the weight of the spoken word.

Oral communication skills are valuable for managers because:

o important concerns get expressed and discussed
o the manager is more persuasive, so more able to win support
o agreement between colleagues is more likely to occur
o misunderstandings are less frequent
o the quality of debate is high, which improves decision making.

You can improve your oral communication skills by obtaining feedback on your personal style. Closed circuit television is a particularly valuable medium. Skills are acquired by practice and review under the guidance of a competent mentor or tutor.

Conclusion

These twelve communication skills can be isolated for analysis but, in reality, they complement each other. Those senior politicians entering Ronald Reagan's oval office knew that they had to be orators, counsellors, trainers and cartoonists. Their personal communication skills could materially affect the wellbeing of millions. Perhaps the lives of us all.

It is fitting to conclude this book with the spotlight on each reader. Some of the topics in the previous chapters are more appropriate for leaders and those who design organizations. This chapter highlights skills that we all need and can begin improving today.

Are inadequate communication skills a blockage in your organization?

The following projects from the companion volume *50 Activities for Unblocking Organizational Communication*, are especially relevant:

44   Manager's communication checklist.
45   Communication skills inventory.
46   Develop your assertion skills.
47   The competent communicator.
48   Attentive listening.
49   Using flipcharts.
50   Personal energy and communication effectiveness.

Index

Index